Reviews of *Creating Superfans*

"Exceptional customer experience is the goal of every smart business-person. *Creating Superfans* gives you not just the playbook for making it happen, but also the play*list*. The smart, simple advice and pop culture references put CX into terms your team will relate to, remember, and—most importantly—really use."

JON ACUFF, *New York Times*-bestselling author, *Soundtracks*

"These pages are filled with powerful stories, specific examples, and a complete framework for turning customers into the engine of your business. I particularly love the section on understanding customers' stories."

JAY BAER, bestselling coauthor, *Talk Triggers*

"I know firsthand what it means to have loyal, dedicated fans. Whatever your 'thing' is, you'll find advice in *Creating Superfans* to help you go further, faster, with a loyal tribe cheering you on."

BOBBY BONES, *New York Times*-bestselling author; TV and radio personality

"*Creating Superfans* contains the secrets your business needs to stand out in a crowd and to attract, engage, and retain your own raving fanbase."

DORIE CLARK, *Wall Street Journal*-bestselling author, *The Long Game*; executive education faculty, Duke University's Fuqua School of Business

"This is the customer experience soundtrack that you'll want to play on repeat for months on end until the ideas, stories, and principles are so embedded in your psyche that creating raving fans will be as easy as 1, 2, 3..."

JOEY COLEMAN, *Wall Street Journal*-bestselling author, *Never Lose a Customer Again*

"Maybe you prefer to spend countless sums on advertising, and countless hours constantly chasing and attaining new customers. Or maybe Brittany Hodak's masterful guide will help you flip that relationship on its head—instead of selling *to* people, you'll create advocates and superfans who do the 'selling' for you."

JEFF HADEN, contributing editor, *Inc.*;
author, *The Motivation Myth*

"*Creating Superfans* is the must-read manual for turning your customers and employees into superfans. If you have customers, you need this book—period."

JOHN HALL, senior contributor, *Forbes*; serial entrepreneur

"There is nothing stronger than third-party advocacy. It's what every marketer wants! But how do you create the elusive 'superfan'? Start with this playbook: fun, accessible, and full of practical ideas you can implement right away. A must-read for any marketer in the digital age."

SHAMA HYDER, bestselling author, *The Zen of Social Media Marketing*; CEO, Zen Media

"When your marketplace is crowded, the ultimate catalyst to conversion is the creation of an army of supporters, fans, and ideally superfans. This book delivers the formula to achieve *exactly* that!"

PHIL M JONES, bestselling author, *Exactly What to Say*

"Brittany Hodak is a master at helping brands connect with their audience in a way that creates deep loyalty and meaningful, authentic bonds. The strategies in *Creating Superfans* are priceless!"

RORY VADEN, *New York Times*-bestselling author;
cofounder, Brand Builders Group

CREATING

**How to Turn
Your Customers Into
Lifelong Advocates**

BRITTANY HODAK
FOREWORD BY SHEP HYKEN

SUPER
FANS

PAGE TWO

Cataloguing in publication information is available from Library and Archives Canada.
ISBN 978-1-77458-078-3 (hardcover)
ISBN 978-1-77458-079-0 (ebook)
ISBN 978-1-77458-080-6 (audiobook)

Page Two
pagetwo.com

Edited by Emily Schultz
Copyedited by Melissa Edwards
Proofread by Alison Strobel
Cover, interior design, and illustrations by Fiona Lee
Printed and bound in Canada by Friesens
Distributed in Canada by Raincoast Books
Distributed in the US and internationally by Macmillan

23 24 25 26 27   5 4 3 2 1

BrittanyHodak.com

This one goes out to my three favorite people:
Jeff, Kadoh, and Jones. I love you!

Contents

Foreword

Same Ol' Situation

Some things in this world are timeless. Expressions like love, music, and storytelling were essential long before any of us were born and will be part of humanity's collective existence forever.

In business, there also exists a set of enduring elements, and two of the most important are word-of-mouth marketing and customer centricity—along with its many subsets, including customer experience, customer service, and customer loyalty and retention.

Brittany Hodak is a customer experience rockstar. And, just like some recording artists burst onto the scene and wow critics and fans with a debut album, Brittany's first book is worthy of a 5-star review. It's like a greatest hits collection you'll want playing on repeat in the minds of everyone on your team.

I met Brittany a few years ago when she spoke to my Entrepreneurs' Organization chapter in Saint Louis and I immediately knew that she "got it." We quickly bonded over our shared love of creating amazing customer experiences. Brittany knows that the importance of customer experience can be traced all the way back to the days of the Old Testament.

Tucked away in the British Museum is a customer complaint letter carved in Akkadian cuneiform that dates to 1750 BCE. It was written by an unsatisfied copper ore customer named Nanni to his supplier, Ea-nasir. The tablet hints that it was not the first correspondence between the two. It reads:

> What do you take me for, that you treat somebody like me with such contempt? I have sent as messengers gentlemen like ourselves to collect the bag with my money (deposited with you) but you have treated me with contempt by sending them back to me empty-handed several times, and that through enemy territory. Is there anyone among the merchants who trade with Telmun who has treated me in this way? . . . I shall exercise against you my right of rejection because you have treated me with contempt.

Yikes! That's a lot of contempt.

If you'll give me a little creative license, I'd like to put together a short mashup of Nanni's letter and a modern-day version of what some companies deem (unfortunately) to be an acceptable customer experience:

> Nanni walks up to the customer service window and puts the product he was shipped down on the counter.
>
> "I received these copper ingots, but they aren't at all like the ones the salesman showed me," Nanni explains calmly.
>
> "Do you have your original receipt or purchase order?" the customer service representative asks.
>
> "Uh, no."
>
> "Then take this clay tablet and bone stylus, sit down over there and cuneiform down all the details."
>
> "Could you just get my rep? It's Ea-nasir. I think he'll be able to straighten this out. I've traveled through a war zone to get here, and I'd really like to take care of this quickly."

"He's away on business, but I'll see what I can do," the rep says. She walks to a back room, where she stands around for a few minutes. Eventually, she returns to the counter.

"The best thing is for you to just fill out the clay tablet. We will review your case and get back to you as soon as the war is over. Next!"

The issues that upset Nanni almost 4,000 years ago are the same ones that irk customers today.

The product he received did not meet his expectations. He sought resolution to his problem several times (including sending messengers through a war zone to ask for a refund!). Had Ea-nasir Fine Copper set things right the first time, the British Museum wouldn't have this interesting artifact to display. The relationship between this buyer and seller would have been quickly restored.

Instead, their relationship is poisoned. Trust and confidence have deteriorated to the point that Nanni will certainly have his eyes open for a new supplier—and will very likely tell his friends and neighbors to do the same.

The best and most-loved brands and businesses understand that human desires are the same now as they were in Nanni's day. Except now, the Nannis of the world aren't chiseling their complaints into clay tablets and sending messengers across the desert on camels—they're sharing them on social media and in other public forums that potential customers all around the world can see *in real time*.

Any customer's feedback, good or bad, can go viral at any moment. One present-day Nanni can shape the perception that millions of people have of you or your business. Even the opinions that don't go viral play a role in whether potential customers will be lining up to do business with you or running in the opposite direction.

Customer experience is timeless, but it's never been timelier. High expectations are the rule, not the exception. It's never been easier for a competitor to tempt your customers with a promise of a better service experience. Regardless of the field you're in, you won't find long-term success without prioritizing your customers . . . period.

Picking up this book was a great decision. An even better decision is ordering copies for every employee at your company and making it required reading. In the pages that follow, Brittany makes the subject of customer experience not only approachable and exciting, but also fun. Whether it's someone's first year at your business or their fiftieth, they will find value in this fantastic field guide, and they'll be so entertained by it that they may not even realize it's educational.

Brittany's SUPER Model is simultaneously simple and spectacular— implement it as she prescribes in your business and you're sure to find not just success, but superfans. Customers shouting or tweeting (or *carving*) complaints? No way. By the end of this book, you'll be on your way to an army of superfan customers cheering you on. Who knows? Maybe your amazing customer experience will become so legendary that someone like me will be writing about it a few millennia from now.

SHEP HYKEN

Customer service/experience expert, Hall of Fame keynote speaker, *New York Times*-bestselling author, and Brittany Hodak superfan

Enterlude

W HAT'S THE first concert you ever attended?

Do you still remember the energy from that night? The crowd, the lights, the songs? Did you go to the show with someone special? Perhaps you went alone but met someone who became a lifelong friend.

My first concert was Matchbox 20. It was 1998, and the band was on the road supporting their seminal debut album, *Yourself or Someone Like You*. My dad drove me and my best friend, Pam, over an hour to the show at Barnhill Arena in Fayetteville, Arkansas, even though it was a school night.

From the first chord of the opening song to the encore performance of "Long Day," I was mesmerized. I never wanted that feeling to end.

Pam and I bought matching shirts at the merch booth and wore them like badges of honor at school the next day. As we recapped the night's magic to friends in our eighth-grade homeroom class that morning, I announced definitively that I was going to work in the music industry one day.

And I did. From a humble beginning as a radio station mascot (the best first job *ever*, by the way), I founded and later sold an entertainment company whose clients included Dolly Parton, KISS,

Taylor Swift, Luke Bryan, Katy Perry, and dozens more of the biggest entertainers on the planet. (But more on that later.)

In the music industry, there are many measures of success for an artist—streaming totals, number-one songs, merchandise sales, and more. But there's one metric that dwarfs the rest: ticket sales.

When an artist goes on tour, how many people are willing to spend their time and money to see them live? Are they a headliner or an opening act? Can they sell out shows in twelve cities or 120?

Now, imagine that *your* most loyal customers are showing up together, city by city, to buy *your* product or service. I know, you might not be an artist. But humor me. How many loyal customers are there? Would they be filling bars, ballrooms, or baseball stadiums?

I've spent most of my career studying fandom: working to understand why some things experience exponential growth while others fail to launch. Why some brands go viral while others go bust. This book is the product of nearly two decades of work and research across many facets of business and pop culture.

Whether we're talking about rockstars or real estate, a brick-and-mortar store or an online business, "superfans" are critically important. They exist in every industry, although they go by different names. Perhaps you call them VIPs, promoters, frequent fliers, advocates, season-ticket holders, or subscribers. They are the customers who will consistently choose you at the exclusion of others . . . and tell their friends—and even strangers—to do the same. The loyal, enthusiastic customers who will keep buying from you again and again.

Think back to junior high. How did you discover new music before algorithms existed to serve up personal suggestions? To start, it was likely a combination of MTV, late-night shows, music magazines, and the radio. Maybe you were lucky enough to live in a town with a fun record store where the clerks always seemed to know about the hottest new thing.

IF YOUR
CUSTOMERS
AREN'T TELLING
★★ THEIR FRIENDS ★★
ABOUT YOU
YOU'RE IN
TROUBLE

And finally—and probably most importantly—you discovered music from your friends. The people around you whose recommendations you trusted because they knew you. Cousins, older siblings, classmates who were cooler than you . . . when they said, "Check this out!" there's a good chance you would, right? Maybe they'd let you borrow a cassette, or they'd burn you a CD. Perhaps you'd buy an entire album based on their feedback, even if you'd only heard one song. That's how I discovered Matchbox 20: it was after a friend in Florida said, "You've got to buy this CD!" (Thanks again, Dana!)

Now, fast forward to today. Where did you turn for advice the last time you needed to buy something new? Product reviews from other customers on Google or Amazon? Maybe you opened your favorite social app to see what influencers had to say. Or maybe you reached out directly to people in your network: online or in-real-life friends whose opinions you trust implicitly.

We're hardwired to believe—and act on—feedback from the people we know, like, and trust. The only thing that's changed over the past few decades is the amount of people we now have easy access to. Word-of-mouth marketing has been around for as long as people have lived on the planet. Why did Adam take a bite of that forbidden fruit? Because Eve told him it was awesome.

A band's fanbase grows in large part because of the superfans who advocate on their behalf. The passion those people feel for the band is contagious. Suddenly a few dozen fans in Omaha become a few hundred, and then a few thousand. Then those fans in Omaha tell their friends in Ohio and Oakland and Oklahoma and, before long, the band is selling out shows in forty cities.

Your brand is no different. Whether you're just getting off the ground or you've been around for fifty years, one thing's for sure: if your customers aren't telling their friends about you, you're in trouble.

Customers rarely, if ever, tell others about an average experience with a product or service—just as people seldom comment on a forgettable song they heard on the radio. These things are filler, helping us pass the time between Point A and Point B. Too many businesses fall into the trap of becoming something lots of people "sort of" like instead of intentionally creating an experience the *right* people can't stop telling their friends about. Don't be filler; be unforgettable.

The good news is that you don't have to have headliner swagger to put some of rock and roll's best-kept marketing secrets into practice for your business. You don't even need to carry a tune.

Whatever it is you do or sell, by the end of this book you'll know everything you need to know about creating superfans of your own. Even if your industry doesn't have its own version of Spotify, you can still trend locally, nationally, or even worldwide—and create more raving fans for your business than you ever imagined possible.

What is the most excellent
thing I can do today?

NEIL PEART

PART 1

THE
SUPER
MODEL

Where It's At

. . . .

*The purpose of a business is to create
a customer who creates customers.*
SHIV SINGH

'VE BEEN obsessed with the phenomenon of fandom for as long as
I can remember.

By age four, I had memorized every line of every episode of
DuckTales.

As soon as I could write, I started sending fan mail to every player
on the Texas Rangers roster... and to the coaches, radio announcers,
and managers.

I was so fixated with NASA that I spent my entire fifth-grade year
trying to teach myself Russian with books from the library, in hopes of
better communicating with my future comrades on the International
Space Station.

Each of these interests played a role in shaping the person I am
today. That's because fandom and identity are intrinsically linked.
The things we love become part of our personal stories and influence
the way we see the world and everyone who lives in it. They play a role
in how and why we form relationships with those around us.

Some fandoms are chosen for us. I grew up in a strict Dr Pepper household: if it wasn't Dr Pepper, we didn't drink it. I'm a third-generation Peanuts superfan, raising fourth-generation fans whose nurseries were decorated with Snoopy-themed artwork, toys, and bedding long before they had a say in the matter.

You may have been born into the fandoms for certain sports teams, or you may have been taught that one brand of toothpaste or tomato sauce is superior to all others. While these connections are interesting, I'm even more interested in the brand decisions we make for ourselves—the products, services, and companies we connect with and take with us throughout our lives.

I'm fascinated by our tendency to self-select the brands, products, professionals, and experiences that we will invite into our personal stories. Why do we love some things but not others?

Over the years, I've found that when brands consistently put customers first, everything else falls into place. Across every demographic and industry, customers pay for products, services, and experiences because of the way they make them feel. Large or small, businesses make more money, find more success, and become more loved when they are unfailingly customer centric. And if those benefits aren't enough, such businesses also become "uncopiable" in their industries, all while enhancing the lives of their employees and customers.

Call It What You Want

According to *Merriam-Webster*, the word "superfan" was first used in 1918 to describe "an extremely enthusiastic or dedicated fan." Yet, when I started saying "superfan" to prospects and customers almost a century later—when launching my first startup in 2011—I was often met with responses like, "You're talking about teenage girls screaming for boy bands, right?" or "Isn't a 'superfan' one of those gamers who lives in his parents' basement?"

I would explain that while, yes, those are extreme examples of superfans, that's not the totality of the term. "Superfans" aren't just fanatics on the enthusiastic fringes of pop culture. In fact, they are all around us, making a huge impact on nearly every sector of the economy. They exist for every category of product and service. They come in all ages and from every background and income bracket. And, while it may not read "superfan" on their government-issued IDs, that's exactly what they are: loyal, enthusiastic advocates whose recommendations influence the actions of those around them.

This book isn't written to help the existing superstars grow their fanbases: it's a manual for the rest of us. A proven, easy-to-implement system that anyone (including *you!*) can put into practice to transform from a potential commodity provider into a category leader in the eyes of your prospects and customers . . . and maybe even a category of one.

Over the past fifteen years, I've worked with brands of all sizes— from early-stage startups to beloved nonprofits to corporate titans like Walmart and Disney—to help their executives, salespeople, marketing teams, product designers, and service representatives create, engage, and multiply superfans.

Creating superfan customers should be a top priority for every businessperson and every brand today. A well-executed superfan strategy is one of the most powerful ways to futureproof any business against competitors and market conditions.

When you see "superfan" in this book, I don't want you to think of people packing a stadium on game day or donning cosplay at Comic-Con. Yes, those are superfans, but not the kind we're going to focus on creating here. Unless, of course, you happen to be a star linebacker or a sci-fi writer. In that case, proceed! For the rest of us, here's what I'm talking about when I say "superfan": *a superfan is a customer*

SUPERFANS

ARE

CUSTOMERS

WHO CREATE

★ MORE ★

CUSTOMERS

or stakeholder who is so delighted by their experience with a brand, product, or service that they become an enthusiastic advocate.

Let's break down the key elements in that definition—the ones that separate true superfans from all other customers. Understanding the difference is critical to identifying your existing superfans and implementing a plan to create more of them.

Money Changes Everything

One qualification for defining someone as a superfan is that they have spent money with your company. They're *a customer or stakeholder,* not just an admirer. This is an important distinction because there is a real-world transactional value to superfandom. While it's true that someone can have an affinity for your brand without first being a customer, they can't advocate in as meaningful a way until a transaction has occurred.

Let's say you ask two friends to recommend an attorney. One enthusiastically recommends someone they have hired on multiple occasions, always with great outcomes. The second friend says their son plays baseball with the son of an attorney who works at a firm nearby. Your friend says, "He seems like a really nice guy!" Whose recommendation are you more likely to act on? The first, obviously.

Why does the first recommendation hold more weight? Because actual customers' feedback is more relevant than feedback from those who *haven't* done business with you. The only caveat here is for any stakeholders who aren't your direct customer but who are involved in transactions with those who are. If you're working in an industry where a third party is often present, both your end customer *and* that intermediary can be superfans.

I Gotta Feeling

. . . .

Customers are the most powerful tool in the world for creating more customers. But not *all* customers. The next key part of my superfan definition is *who is so delighted by their experience*. If you want some-one to become a superfan, their experience must be outstanding—or, at the very least, it must exceed their expectations.

I'll never forget a question posed to me when I was applying for my first trademark. My attorney asked, "Is this a product business or a service business?"

I said, "It's both." He told me the U.S. Patent and Trademark Office would require that I choose one or the other. I was stumped. "They're interconnected," I argued. "The services I provide will very often culminate in a product being produced." At the time, most of my projects involved consulting with recording artists and then creating physical collectible items for their fans—things like limited-edition boxed sets, coffee-table books, and so on. But my clients were coming to me because of my expertise. The service behind those products.

In the years since, I've become an even firmer believer that the "product or service" distinction is irrelevant. We've seen the rise of the SaaS (software as a service) model, which announces right in its name that what was once widely considered a product (software) is now a service. I can't recall if I checked the "product" or "service" box more than a decade ago, but I do remember doing so under protest and arguing that the USPTO should update its applications to reflect the fact that the line between these two worlds blurred long ago into a single, all-important category: *experience*.

We're living in an experience economy. The experience your customers have with your brand or business is the most important competitive advantage you have at your disposal. When you get it right, it's the hardest thing for competitors to copy. Experience is baked into the DNA of your company... and into all of the products and services you offer.

Customer experience, or CX, is the term for the way a customer feels about the totality of their interactions with a brand or business, from start to finish. I love the term, because "experience" is doing a lot of work. For starters, it's both singular and plural. While the experience of every customer is important, "customer experience" also refers to the sum of the experiences of all customers—for example: "That business is known for its amazing customer experience."

"Experience" is also both a verb and a noun. It's something people receive (noun), but that they're also actively participating in (verb). Pretty cool, right? (Shout-out to all my fellow grammar nerds!)

Think of your own favorite brands. It's likely that the experience is part of the draw. Up to 86 percent of customers are willing to pay more money for a great customer experience.

If you're a solopreneur, you may oversee the totality of customer experience, before and after a sale takes place. If you're a leader, your team may oversee parts, but not all, of the customer journey. If you work at a larger enterprise, you may be responsible for only a small fraction of a very big picture.

The best professionals know that, even if they're only directly responsible for one part of the customer's experience, they must understand every part of it intimately. To a customer, it doesn't matter if you work in sales, support, product design, shipping, accounting, marketing, legal, or another department entirely. Whoever you are, you're representing the *company*. No irate customer has ever said, "Oh, a *different* department was responsible for this error? Okay, then. I'm no longer upset. Thanks for your help!" Karen doesn't care what department you work in—she just wants her problem (real or perceived) fixed. She also doesn't care how long you've worked there. If you're wearing the name tag (literal or metaphorical), you're in the hot seat.

Tell Your Friends
. . . .

Now let's examine the final part of my "superfan" definition: *they become an enthusiastic advocate.* Superfan customers are eager to share stories about their experiences with a brand. They don't talk because they're being paid or incentivized in some way by an agreement with your company. They tell people about you because they *want* to.

Superfandom is real, authentic enthusiasm from true supporters. This is the kind of unprompted, unfiltered feedback for which audiences used to turn to the world of so-called "social-media influencers," before advertisers, bots, and bad actors depleted almost every shred of trust and credibility from it.

I'm not arguing that there's no role for influencers in your marketing mix, because there very well may be. Just know that when the word "superfan" appears in this book, it's not meant to encompass any partner whose relationship with your brand is tied to a financial agreement with terms on both sides. Plus, most influencers are over-hyped anyway. As it turns out, almost everyone is an influencer—or a micro-influencer, at the least.

It's true: 93 percent of consumers say an online review has influenced their purchase decision. And 91 percent of 18- to 34-year-olds trust online reviews as much as personal recommendations. You create superfans by being so exceptional that customers can't help but talk about you. Our hyperconnected world makes it virtually impossible for remarkable products, services, and experiences to go unnoticed for long.

Did you catch the word "remarkable" in there? It's a biggie. Ever wonder why there are so few 3-star reviews in the world, but so many 1- and 5-star reviews? When we have an amazing experience or a terrible experience, we talk about it. But an ordinary one? When was the last time you were out with a friend and said, "I've got to tell you about this new restaurant—it was just okay"? Luckily, this book will help you go *beyond* remarkable, all the way to SUPER.

I Like the Sound of That

Put simply, brands that learn to harness the power of fandom are unstoppable. Identity is a powerful thing. Once a customer identifies as a fan of something, it becomes part of the fabric of their everyday life. As cultural anthropologist Susan Kresnicka noted in *Variety*:

> When we define ourselves as fans, we do more—we watch more, share more, buy more, evangelize more, participate more, help more.

If you do your job correctly, your customers will talk about you. Learning to engage your customers doesn't just get them talking (and, more importantly, get their friends listening)—it makes them feel a sense of ownership in your brand. Your story becomes part of their story.

Speaking of ownership, I hope that by the end of this book you'll have made the concepts you are about to read your own! If you're anything like me, recaps help you remember information longer and put it into practice more quickly. That's why every chapter in this book ends with a "Superquick! Rewind" refresher.

Want even more? Visit BrittanyHodak.com/SUPER for the free Creating Superfans Playbook, plus videos and printable resources to help accelerate and amplify the adoption of this book's principles across your entire organization.

◄◄ SUPERQUICK! REWIND ◄◄

A superfan is a customer or stakeholder who is so delighted by their experience with a brand, product, or service that they become an enthusiastic advocate. Advocates are the new influencers. Treat every customer like they alone have the power to make or break your brand—because they do.

We're living in an experience economy. Customers will pay more to do business with brands that provide exceptional experiences. CX is one of the most powerful ways to futureproof your brand and one of the easiest ways to ensure that more customers come back and become loyal advocates.

2

I Don't Care

. . . .

Build something 100 people love,
not something 1 million people kind of like.
BRIAN CHESKY

N OW THAT we've covered superfans, let's look at the other side of the coin. I'm not talking about "haters," or customers whose less-than-ideal experience has compelled them to leave a negative review or to direct would-be customers to your competitors. Unhappy customers can be highly valuable, because you can learn a great deal from their complaints.

Just as it's been said that the opposite of love is not hate but indifference, the opposite of superfandom is not hate but apathy. The "meh" crowd. Would-be customers—or, worse, *actual* customers—who just don't care enough to care one way or the other.

When I consult with new clients, they often tell me they have an awareness problem: not enough people know about their amazing brand and the wonderful products and services they sell.

This is sometimes the case, but much more often I find that *lots* of qualified prospects and leads are aware of them. Many of these people have even considered them before, but didn't convert.

Even worse, some customers who *did* make a purchase just weren't wowed. The product was fine; the service was okay. It was all very... forgettable. Ordinary. And so, when the time came to purchase again, they rolled the dice and tried another solution.

Very often, stagnant growth is not an awareness problem at all. It's an apathy problem.

Comfortably Numb

Apathy is one of the most underrated problems in business today. It doesn't get a ton of press, but it should. Companies of all sizes allocate nearly immeasurable resources—dollars, time, energy, and ideas among them—to chasing new customers. Then, when they've got those customers, they do an *okay* job of taking care of their needs. Naturally, customers get apathetic and think, "Maybe I'll see what else is out there."

I was a Brownie in the Girl Scouts for a year and I remember singing a song that went, "Make new friends, but keep the old. One is silver, and the other gold." The same is true for your existing (aka "old") customers—except, in many cases, they can mean *literal* gold.

It takes less time, effort, and money to sell something *more* to an existing customer than to sell *anything* to a new customer. You can't afford to let your customers become numb, comfortably or otherwise. Apathy drives attrition and eats away at your profits. If you're not paying attention, your customers can shrug and move on with their lives. And the same goes for prospects, who can move on before they've even given you the proper time of day.

There has never been so much competition for human attention, and getting someone to care about *your* thing has never been so challenging. I'm busy, you're busy, we're all busy. That's where the distinction between "awareness" and "apathy" sometimes gets blurred.

We're living with more distractions than at any point in human history, and we're being inundated with more messages competing for our attention than ever before (tens of thousands, by some estimates). Yet we still find a way to make time for the things we really care about. There is no such thing as "too busy"—only too uninterested.

How many times have you said, "I'm so busy" (and meant it), only to find time the same day to watch TV or play a game or relax with a book? We make time for the things that matter. Whatever you're promoting or selling, the right message—let's call it an "apathy buster"—will help you catapult past the noise and command the attention of the people you care about most. At least initially. Then, it's up to your customer experience to keep them engaged.

I bet you can think of lots of things that you never cared about . . . until you did. Maybe a friendly salesperson persuaded you to try a new product that's become one of your staples. Or, maybe a brand's message made you care (or care *more*) about something for the first time because you identified with that mission or purpose. Or, maybe, you had a firsthand experience with a product that worked so well you now wonder how you ever lived without it. (I'm lookin' at you, Mr. Clean Magic Erasers!) Something made you care. You went from apathy to advocacy. Let's look closely at that journey and how you can use it to create—and *keep*—superfans.

The Climb

There are dozens of giant, low-quality stuffed animals cluttering my kids' playroom, all serving as proof of my lifelong love of carnival games. From ring toss and balloon darts to milk jugs and water pistols, there's virtually nothing on a midway I won't stop to play.

One of the few games I've never been able to master, although I've tried more times than I care to admit, is the rope ladder. You know the one. It's anchored at a single point at the top and bottom, and the objective is to climb from the bottom rung to the top without losing your balance and bellyflopping onto the inflatable pillow below while strangers point and laugh.

That rope ladder is the perfect metaphor for customer apathy. Way up at the top, on the final rung, is advocacy. That's where you want your customers to reach. But first, they've got to make it past apathy.

And apathy isn't just the first rung. It's also the giant cushion underneath that customers can fall down into. It's the other games and rides and funnel cakes that can distract prospects before they even venture onto your ladder. As if that weren't enough, the workings of apathy are causing that ladder to swing, challenging the equilibrium of every would-be climbing champion.

Much like falling off a rope ladder, customer apathy can happen at any moment, on any point of the climb—even when you least expect it. Advancing from one rung to the next is never guaranteed and should never be taken for granted.

Let's take a closer look at the dangers of customer apathy and what I like to think of as the Ladder to Superfandom.

Apathy

Recall that ladder image in your mind, and consider its base and everything around it to be apathy. Some people will be apathetic to your brand, specifically. Others will be indifferent to the entire category in which you operate. Fine. Don't worry about them. Your thing is not going to be right for everyone, and that's okay. The sooner

ADVOCACY

AFFINITY

ADOPTION

ACTION

ATTRACTION

AWARENESS

APATHY

you acknowledge that, the more quickly you can move on to more valuable prospects. Your job is simply to help shepherd the people who *do* care further up the ladder.

Why is "apathy" at the bottom instead of "anger" or "dissatisfaction"? Remember: even anger has value—far more than apathy. If someone has engaged with your brand enough to become angry, there's a good chance they have useful feedback to offer. Or, they could just be the wrong fit—at which point anger will likely soon fade to annoyance, ambivalence, or . . . you guessed it: apathy. We'll talk more about dealing with angry customers in Chapter 13.

Apathy at play: Remember that your customers can fall off the ladder at any point in their climb toward superfandom. For each rung I'm about to describe, I've laid out the key triggers and warning signs to look for, so you can help your customers regain their balance before it's too late.

Awareness

Next up is awareness. If you've ever watched someone try to scale a carnival rope ladder (or if you've tried it yourself), you know that getting from the first rung to the second is relatively simple, because you're still close to the ground. The same is true for awareness.

Awareness is one of the easiest metaphorical steps in the process. Put simply, it's when someone knows that you exist. If you've got a great product and a strong message (Part 2 of this book will help you nail the second), finding people to pay attention is relatively simple.

It's never been easier to reach hyper-targeted audiences through advertising than it is today, especially online. By niching down into almost countless layers, you can land in the inboxes or social feeds of the people who fit the *exact* demographic and psychographic profile you want to talk to. For every person on the internet, it seems, there's a company offering you the opportunity to reach them. It's nothing new: there are plenty of offline opportunities to micro-target, too. Big data has been big business for decades.

Paying to generate awareness beyond your ideal market is often pointless. That's why smart marketers will bet on 10,000 engaged fans over 1 million casual followers any day—and Part 3 of this book will help you get clarity on exactly whom to target. Your time and efforts will be much better spent thinking about moving customers up the perilous steps still ahead of them.

Apathy at play: What does apathy look like at the awareness step? People whose reaction to hearing your message is, "I just don't care." It might be a case of the wrong person for your message, or the right person at the wrong time. Either way, apathy kicks in almost immediately and your story becomes one of the tens of thousands of messages that a prospective customer's brain ignores every day. It didn't connect with their story. You've become noise, not signal.

Attraction

Attraction is the next rung up the ladder. This is when someone has given you their information but not their money. You have their interest and, if things go your way, you can move them to "action." Think of it like spotting someone at a bar (or in an app) and feeling a spark. There's an attraction . . . or at least a willingness to learn more.

At this stage, you need to show your prospect or customer targeted attention. Everyone is busy. Even if they care about your thing, it's easy for them to forget or get sidetracked. If it seems hard to sustain a customer's interest, try a few different methods of connecting with them in order to get a verbal "yes," "no," or "not now." Remember: "no" today isn't a "no" forever. Show every prospect that you care about them and want their business, and there's a chance they'll come back . . . and an even better chance that they'll remember how you made them feel. Your story is also key in the attraction phase—we'll cover that more deeply in Part 2.

Apathy at play: Did someone unsubscribe from your email list before they made a purchase? Someone asked you for an estimate, and then you never heard back? They cared *almost* enough to become a customer, but not quite. Whether it's because the timing isn't right or because of some other issue, apathy stops your prospect from advancing to the next rung of the ladder.

Action

Ahh, action. That coveted conversion when a prospect shows you the money! The action rung represents the first time someone pays money for your product or service. They've officially graduated from "prospect" to "customer"—congrats! Just don't celebrate too long, because it's still a long way up to "advocacy" and, if you're not careful, the ladder will start to get shaky.

This is where it's critical to remind a customer why they chose you in the first place. If you're in a high-touch business, reach out personally to get details about what their experience was like and tell them you're dedicated to making their *next* experience even better. If your volume of customers is too high to reach out personally, use automation to give them a feeling of personal interaction. Perhaps you can send a video and an invitation to offer feedback (via a short survey or review), along with a highly personalized offer for their next purchase, such as 15 percent off if they re-order within a set period of time.

Here and everywhere, knowledge is power. What percentage of your customers don't come back again after their first purchase? Knowing your average customer purchase cycle and when and why customer attrition is happening is key to moving customers past this perilous step to the ones above it. How would your business change if every customer who *didn't* make a repeat purchase in the past year (or whatever period of time represents your purchase cycle) decided to come back and do business with you again? Focus on getting the *second* conversion from one-time customers and you'll be well on your way to earning the kind of loyalty businesses dream of. It's far easier and less expensive to sell something to an existing customer than a new one.

Apathy at play: How many times have you tried a product or brand, liked it, and then just never bought it again? If you're like most people, probably too many to count. Maybe you got busy and forgot. Maybe you tried another brand that you liked even better. Maybe you just didn't care enough to drive back to the specialty store that you know carries it. Attrition is a real problem for many companies—especially those that are focused on acquiring customers instead of creating superfans.

Adoption

When apathy doesn't creep in after the first purchase, customers advance to the adoption rung. I define adoption as when a customer has spent money with your brand at least twice. Customers are beginning to embrace your product or service and have now had multiple experiences with your brand. At some point soon, they'll decide they like your brand enough to move to the next rung, or they'll decide that you're okay, but not spectacular. At that point, they'll look for another partner. Your job, obviously, is to help them advance further up the ladder.

If you're in a business where the results are somewhat subjective— maybe you're operating a restaurant or a hair salon or a personal-training gym—it's important for a customer's second experience to be *at least* as amazing as the first so they know it wasn't a fluke. This reinforces their choice and signals that future experiences are likely to be enjoyable, too.

In music, people use the term "sophomore slump" to describe a second album that fails to reach the same commercial or critical acclaim as a debut album. Many artists fall victim to it. They can deliver something exceptional once, but not again. Don't let your business become a one-hit wonder. Make the second experience, and all that follow it, just as magical as the first. Pretty soon, your customers will be playing you on repeat.

Apathy at play: Very few unhappy customers take the time to complain to a business. Instead, the majority simply leave. No suggestions, no opportunities given to address their grievances. They just bounce like bored coeds at a party when the keg's empty. This often happens even after the adoption stage. Sometimes it's because the first experience was solid, but the second was shaky. Instead of rolling the dice for a third time, customers decide to give another company the opportunity to provide a more consistent experience.

Affinity

They like you—they really like you! Affinity is oh-so-close to the top of the ladder. Once you've got a customer on this rung, they're likely pretty loyal. They may be part of a frequent-customer club, and it's very unlikely that they're rate-shopping against your competitors. You've won them over.

Many consumer packaged goods products find that their customers tend to hang out on the affinity rung. I *like* a lot of the products that I buy again and again, but I'm not going out of my way to recommend them. The brand has my loyalty, for the most part, but not necessarily my enthusiasm, and certainly not my advocacy.

Affinity is also a frequent ladder rung for B2B and B2B2C salespeople and professionals. A customer *likes* her wealth manager, or a realtor *likes* a particular title agent. You've got a good thing going, but they don't feel that enthusiasm or loyalty... which means they're a flight risk when a more passionate competitor starts showing them the love.

So: always treat repeat customers at least as well as you treat those first-time customers you're courting so aggressively.

Apathy at play: Often, apathy wins out over affinity because another brand is trying harder to entice your existing customers than you're trying to keep them. Don't give competitors the chance to swoop in! Even if one of your customers ignores the first few offers from a competitor, if they aren't feeling the love from you, there's a chance that curiosity (and apathy!) will kick in and they'll give that competitor a try. If they find the grass is indeed greener, they might not be back.

Advocacy

And, finally, there's advocacy. These customers have felt the love from you, and they love you back. Well done! You've successfully led them to the top of the ladder through an environment rife with threats. Do a little dance while you belt out "Started from the Bottom" in their honor.

What's the difference between affinity and advocacy? Amplification. Advocates aren't just loyal, they're *vocal*. They share the experience they've had with your brand with others, which attracts more customers. That advocacy may be structured or unstructured. It may be scheduled or sporadic. It might happen online or *in* line, at a bank or a bar or a baseball game. Chances are, it's a mix of all the above. These are the customers who create more customers. Those superfans we're working so hard to create.

WHAT'S THE DIFFERENCE BETWEEN AFFINITY AND ADVOCACY?

AMPLIFICATION

Apathy at play: Think you're safe when your fans get to the advocacy stage? Think again. It's not like the board game Sorry!, where getting your game pieces to "Home" means you've got nothing else to worry about. Apathy can still kick in. It's the threat that never ends. Your most loyal customers—even those who are vocal advocates—can lose interest . . . typically, when your story and theirs are no longer in sync.

Can't Stop, Won't Stop

Once someone becomes a superfan of your brand, it's still critical to show them the love. In fact, superfan customers can be even more likely to feel slighted when things don't go their way. Because these superfans have been loyal and feel personally invested in the success of the company, lapses in service can create outsized negative impacts.

Country star Granger Smith once told me that every member of his touring staff has been trained to give extra attention to fans who have visible tattoos inspired by him, his music, or his beloved alter ego, Earl Dibbles, Jr.

In the early days of Granger's career, anyone spotted with such a tattoo got instant VIP service: backstage passes, a meet-and-greet with the band, and very likely some merch from Granger's popular Yee Yee Apparel brand.

"Can you imagine how terrible it would be to have a tattoo of an artist you like, and then go to their show and a member of their team treats you like a jerk?" he asked. "That would be the only thing you thought about when you saw that tattoo from then on. And, since it's on your body, you're basically screwed."

Your loyal customers might not have literal tattoos, but many feel an emotional connection to your brand. Don't make them feel like they mean less to you than you mean to them. Take care of them, or those tattoos could turn to scars. The last thing you want is formerly loyal customers running up and down the proverbial boardwalk, telling people who haven't even reached the midway that they shouldn't bother trying to climb your rope ladder because you don't care either way if they make it to the top.

◀◀ SUPERQUICK! REWIND ◀◀

When it comes to your brand, every customer starts at the apathy stage. Your job is to give them a boost, and advance them up the Ladder to Superfandom: awareness, attraction, action, adoption, affinity, and finally advocacy. But remember! Just because they have moved up the ladder, that doesn't mean the risk is over. Apathy can interrupt the journey at any point, so never let your guard down.

3

Brand New Set of Rules

. . . .

*It's easier to love a brand
when the brand loves you back.*
SETH GODIN

A S MUCH AS you'd like to think your brand is totally within your control—the clever ad campaigns and social slogans and punchy website copy—the reality is that the employees representing your brand are a *huge* part of the equation. That's because your brand isn't what you say it is. It's what your customers say it is, and their interactions with your employees represent some of the most tangible, memorable experiences they will have with your brand.

You may be thinking, "I don't believe that. People are superfans of brands because of the products the brand makes, not the people who work for the brand." In some instances, you're right. Diehard sneaker-heads may overlook a bad experience in a Nike store because they're so brand loyal. So, too, might someone who's been giving money to Apple for more than half their life, or who spent years waiting to take that perfect family trip to Disney World.

Here is what I would (kindly) say to you: your brand probably isn't Nike or Apple or Disney... yet. And until you get there, a huge part of the perception customers will have of your brand is based on interactions with representatives of your company. If you're not yet at the point where your logo evokes an emotional response, then it's up to your employees to make your customers feel something.

Not just *some* employees, by the way. This isn't a C-suite thing. Every person representing your brand has the power to make or break a first impression... or a fiftieth. Remember *Fast Times at Ridgemont High*? Judge Reinhold's character, Brad Hamilton, was All American Burger's employee of the month when he fumbled an interaction with an irate customer. Part of the reason Brad became flustered was because he was filling in for his buddy. But here's the thing: your customers don't care if it's someone's first day on the job or their five hundredth. They just want to have their expectations met... or, preferably, exceeded.

When a customer's expectations aren't met, they often can't tell if the failure is a process problem or a people problem—and they don't really care. They just blame the brand and move on. That's what I did when I attempted to buy a Costco membership and instead left with a lifetime supply of Kirkland-branded apathy.

What's in Store for Me

Costco is a membership-only wholesale store, so customers need a card to shop there. There were no Costco stores near me when I was growing up, so I had never been inside of one until my husband and I moved to Tennessee. I figured that our new suburban lifestyle meant we should belong to at least one wholesale club (after all, we suddenly had a big, mostly empty house crying out for bulk packages of paper towels), so one Saturday morning we decided to visit both Costco and Sam's Club and sign up at one or both businesses.

When we walked into Costco, I told the employee at the door that we would like to look around and then sign up for a membership.

He scoffed, "We don't allow window shopping," then directed me to the customer service desk. After a ten-minute wait, I repeated my request at the desk, telling the clerk that I had never been to a Costco and would like to look around. Once again, I was told that this was not allowed. I was a little annoyed, but said, "Okay, fine. I would like a membership, please."

The employee asked me a series of questions (directed by prompts on her computer) that were designed to upsell me add-ons: Did I need new tires? Eyeglasses? How about a Disney cruise? I should really consider the Executive membership level.

Finally, after a litany of questions and choices (and her unhidden disdain at my decision to start with the entry-level membership and no extras), it was time to pay. I looked at my phone and saw that it had been twenty-seven minutes since we first walked inside the store.

I handed her my Amex for what I hoped was finally the last step.

She frowned and said, "Oh, we only take Visa."

That would've been nice to know at the beginning. I checked my debit card and, luckily, it was a Visa. As I handed it to her, she said, "You should really apply for a Costco Visa credit card."

I politely told her no, and she told me how much I would regret not having one when I inevitably decided to opt for that Disney cruise and Executive membership.

That was the final straw. I said, "I'm done. I don't want to be a member here." We left the store and drove straight to Sam's to sign up. Six years later, we've easily spent five figures at Sam's . . . and

$0 at Costco. I will probably never have a Costco membership, because I felt both unwelcomed by the employees and inconvenienced by the process.

Bad first impressions are difficult for customers to forget. It's far easier for apathy to kick in when customers don't have much skin in the game—especially when they can quickly find a suitable alternative.

The A Team

Your brand isn't just your logo or your products. To a customer, *every* employee represents the brand. It's whoever seats them at the table when they walk in for lunch. Whoever takes them for a demo ride at the dealership. Whoever handles their paperwork and payment before their appointment. To many leaders, this reality is both exhilarating and a tad frightening. It also underscores the importance of striving not just for superfan *customers*, but superfan *employees*. (You'll find much more about how to create those in Chapter 18.)

Someone recently offered me this unsolicited opinion of treadmills: "You never see anyone in shape on a treadmill. Fit people run outside, where there's fresh air and scenery. You know who you see on treadmills? Fat people."

This hot take would have been eyebrow-raising enough from anyone, but it was especially mind-bending considering the source: the guy delivering my new treadmill!

That's right, immediately after he hoisted the several-hundred-pound exercise machine up a flight of stairs and down a hallway, he shared that wisdom with me.

I looked at him for a few seconds, trying to figure out if he was joking. He wasn't. He went on to tell me that he *never* uses treadmills, even though he's got "a sick company discount" and belongs to

★ ★ ★ ★ **YOUR** ★ ★ ★ ★

BRAND

— **ISN'T JUST** —

YOUR LOGO

a twenty-four-hour gym. In fact, he said, he *only* runs outside . . . at least thirty miles every week, even when it's snowing or 100 degrees.

Then, almost as an afterthought, he added, "You're not big though. Why did you buy an expensive treadmill? Do you have a fat husband or something? Either way, you should just run outside."

I would've assumed he worked for a third-party delivery company if it wasn't for the logo on his shirt. I didn't ask how long he'd been at the company, or why he took a job delivering and assembling treadmills. I just thanked him for his help and said goodbye.

Isn't it fascinating how one employee's performance can shape someone's entire perception of a brand? Now, every time I see the NordicTrack logo, all I think about is that delivery man. I've told the story to dozens of friends (not to mention thousands of strangers from stages and on the internet), and it has impacted the way some of them think about the brand, too.

Your brand's reputation is being shaped every day, in every interaction with every customer. Any employee can be responsible for the first (and maybe last!) impression someone forms about your brand. The stakes are high, so let's talk about how to get it right.

◀◀ SUPERQUICK! REWIND ◀◀

Your brand is an ever-changing entity whose reputation is shaped by the interactions your customers have with your employees every day, online and off. Everyone representing your business is a member of the experience department. It's not just about the stuff you sell—it's about the *experience* surrounding it.

4

This Is How We Do It

. . . .

Do what you do so well that they will
want to see it again and bring their friends.
WALT DISNEY

W HEN MY husband, Jeff, and I began telling our friends and family we were expecting a baby, I was surprised by how many asked, "What are you doing for the gender reveal?"

It was 2017, when—although they were popular—gender-reveal parties weren't quite the crashing-airplanes, blowing-up-cannons, setting-forests-on-fire soirees they've now become.

Two years before *The Atlantic* published an article titled "How Many People Have to Die Before We're Done with Gender Reveals?" (with a subhead that read, "Sadly, this is not a hypothetical question"), I was becoming increasingly annoyed with my friends' incessant questions about something that I considered to be a total waste of energy. These conversations went something like this:

Well-meaning friend #1: What are you doing for your gender reveal?

Me: Won't the doctor just tell me? We're paying a lot for this pregnancy, and it seems like that detail should be included.

Well-meaning friend #2: Have you decided when you're having your gender reveal yet?

Me: I am growing a human being inside my body! Why isn't that enough? This is an example of society expecting too much from women.

Well-meaning friend #3: You should really do your gender reveal as soon as possible so that you can start decorating your nursery and registering for your baby shower!

Me: So once I complete this task, I'll be rewarded by two more difficult-sounding tasks I don't want to do? And I'll still be throwing up three times a day? Awesome!

Luckily, Jeff had a better attitude about this than me. "C'mon," he urged. "It might be fun. Let's do something that doesn't involve us planning a party. What if we asked a celebrity to open the envelope for us?"

I said I could get on board for that idea, but he should choose the celebrity. He said the name before I even finished my sentence: "Jim Harbaugh!"

Jim Harbaugh is the coach of the University of Michigan football team, but he's no typical coach. He's like the archetype of the Perfect College Football Coach™. His dad was a football coach at Michigan in the 1970s, so Jim and his siblings grew up running around the field in Ann Arbor. A decade later, Jim enrolled at the University of Michigan and became the team's star quarterback.

He went on to play in the NFL before super-successful coaching stints in college football and in the NFL. By the time Jeff and I started dating in 2008, Michigan's football program began a string of unsuccessful seasons and lost its luster. In late 2014, after two short-tenured coaches, the program was looking for a new leader to come in and turn things around. When rumors started flying that Michigan's favorite son might be open to the idea of leaving the NFL to take the job, the Wolverine faithful began crossing their fingers.

Shirts saying "Ann Arbaugh" sold out almost instantly. College kids and alums alike started sporting Jim's pant style of choice, khakis. Bloggers were monitoring flight manifests and real estate listings by the hour to look for clues about Harbaugh visits to Ann Arbor.

When it was announced that Coach Harbaugh had, in fact, accepted the job at Michigan, millions of fans—including my husband—went crazy.

Jeff grew up in Michigan. Jim Harbaugh was the quarterback at the very first live game Jeff's father took him to see. Those happy memories helped lay the foundation for Jeff to enroll at the University of Michigan a decade later.

During our years together, I had accompanied Jeff to dozens of Michigan games. Every fall, we crisscrossed the U.S. watching the team play.

For all of these reasons, when Jeff suggested Jim Harbaugh, my heart sank.

"Wonderful," I thought. "Now, in addition to everyone bugging me about this dumb gender reveal, I'm going to have to deal with a husband who will be heartbroken when his hero doesn't write back to him."

I kept my skepticism to myself and said, "Great idea!"

We didn't know Jim Harbaugh. Undeterred, we sent him a letter anyway. After all, we were at least relatively sure which building on campus his office was in.

We wrote a note saying how much fun we'd had at Michigan games over the years and asked if Coach Harbaugh would be kind enough

★ ★ YOU CAN'T BUY ★ ★

SUPERFANS

★ ★ YOU CAN ONLY ★ ★

CREATE THEM

to, in any fashion he chose, let us know the gender of our baby. We included a "letter of intent" from our baby-to-be. Letters of intent are what high school players sign when they commit to teams. We included some cute puns, signed the letter "Baby Hodak," and put it in an envelope, along with the sealed ultrasound picture.

Even though I'd heard anecdotally that Coach Harbaugh is a nice guy, I didn't expect any reply. I'm guessing college football coaches are pretty busy. That's why I asked the ultrasound tech for a second sealed copy of the photo. I planned to open it in a couple of weeks so I could put all of this "gender reveal" nonsense behind me and move on to more important things, like finding pants I could fit into.

I was shocked when I saw a letter in our mailbox a few days later with a University of Michigan logo. I thought it was a coincidence until I saw "Harbaugh" scrawled above the return address. I Facetimed Jeff so we could open it together. We were stunned to find a handwritten note that read:

> Baby Hodak,
>
> I have carefully studied the information from your mom and dad, Jeff and Brittany, and on behalf of the University of Michigan am offering you a 2035 scholarship. Hopefully, with "God willing and the creek not rising," I will be here to coach you.
>
> "Go Blue"
> JIM HARBAUGH

I hadn't even been counting on a reply—I was *definitely* not expecting a handwritten scholarship offer! And while I was excited to know that my little boy was (probably) the youngest recruit in college sports history, I was even more thrilled at the acknowledgment the letter represented.

Someone who had never even met us did something truly kind and meaningful for no personal gain, despite what I assume is an endless list of to-dos. It was an amazing gesture that meant the world to us.

More Than a Feeling

The moment I received that note, I became a University of Michigan football superfan. One card was more effective at turning me into a loyal Wolverine than all the years I'd spent going to Michigan games and tailgates and pep rallies, because it connected *my* story to the *team's* story. A real, tangible connection . . . not a connection through marriage. The halo effect meant I was immediately a superfan of not just Coach Harbaugh and the team, but of *everything* at the University of Michigan. Why? Because that's what he represented—just like you and every one of your colleagues are representing your company.

A few quick internet searches revealed that we were far from the first family Coach Harbaugh had gone out of his way to show kindness to. I found several stories about him sending notes, game balls, and other gifts to fans' weddings, christenings, and bar mitzvahs. He's not some untouchable celebrity whose schedule is too packed to acknowledge people; he's a man of character who leads by example, even when no one is watching.

There are several instances of Jim Harbaugh connecting his story with fans' stories publicly, too—often with many fans simultaneously. My favorite example is a tweet he sent a few days after Halloween one year. It was a photo of himself standing beside a dry-erase board filled with photos of people who'd dressed as him for Halloween. There were about a hundred pictures, featuring fans of all ages decked out in his trademark khakis, Michigan hat, and various maize and blue ensembles. His tweet read: "Great to see people attacking Halloween with an enthusiasm unknown to mankind! #GoBlue." Harbaugh fans recognize the phrase as one of the coach's favorite mantras.

How did every person who saw themselves in that image feel? The same way Jeff and I felt when we got that letter in the mail. Like they were part of something bigger. Like they were *seen*. Sharing that tweet, and others like it, likely secured more goodwill with those fans than any amount of advertising ever could have.

The best marketing doesn't cost anything. You can't buy superfans— you can only *create* them.

If you're thinking, "It's not scalable to send personalized notes to every prospect or customer, and I'm not a celebrity," let me offer a few thoughts.

On the first point, it is possible to send handwritten notes at scale. There are plenty of tech solutions, AI and otherwise, that automate outreach. You can also leverage technology to take other things off your plate to give you more time to write notes. Several successful leaders I know time-block thirty minutes to an hour in their calendars every day to share gratitude, either in written form or in emails. And you can delegate or outsource the more annoying aspects of hand- written notes (shopping for cards, looking up addresses, writing the envelopes, adding stamps, and so on).

And on the second point, you don't have to be a celebrity to make an impact. The power lies in showing people you care about them by taking the time to acknowledge them in some way.

SUPER Model

You're going to see this next point repeated several times throughout this book. That's because it's critically important to remember it. I want it so etched into your brain that you think about it randomly, when you're brushing your teeth or stopped at a red light. You ready? Here goes:

Superfans are created at the intersection of *your* story and *every customer's* story.

YOUR STORY   THEIR STORY

WHERE THE SUPERFAN
MAGIC HAPPENS

They are forged at that magical, overlapping point where it becomes obvious that you share a common purpose or passion. *Your thing* matters and is relevant to *their thing*.

That core principle is the foundation of a five-step system called the SUPER Model that I've taught to thousands of leaders over the past decade. It's helped small-business owners grow their annual revenue from under $100,000 to more than $10,000,000, and it's inspired leaders at Fortune 500 brands how to reframe the way they think about customer experience. You're going to learn it, but first you need to internalize this truth: superfans are created at the intersection of your story and every customer's story.

The SUPER Model is powerful. And, like most powerful models for change, it is simple by design. Simple to remember, simple to teach to your team, and simple to implement, measure, and refine as needed. That's right, *this* SUPER Model gets even better over time. It's like the Heidi Klum of customer experience frameworks.

If you want to create superfans, being great is no longer good enough. You've got to be SUPER:

S	U	P	E	R
Start with Your Story	Understand Your Customer's Story	Personalize	Exceed Expectations	Repeat

The rest of this book is going to teach you to do just that. Here's a quick look at what's coming.

S | Start with your story

Why *start* with your story? Because your clearly defined story is your superpower. It's what helps you go from a potential commodity in the minds of your customers and prospects to a category of one.

In Part 2 of this book, you'll get laser-focused on exactly how to shape and share your story. What sets you apart from every competitor, current and future? What's that secret sauce that no one could copy? Getting clarity on your story is one of the most powerful (and profitable) exercises you can undertake, and the benefits will last a lifetime.

U | Understand your customer's story

You remember where superfans are created, right? At the intersection of your story and every customer's story. So, after getting clear on your story, the next step is to turn your attention to that of your customer.

Any good marketer will tell you that when you try to attract everyone, you end up engaging no one. And yet that's what so many brands and businesspeople do: craft forgettable messages for mass consumption by large, general audiences. In Part 3 of this book, you're going to learn a better way. I'll teach you a foolproof formula that will help you get closer to your customers than ever before.

P | Personalize

The third step of the SUPER Model is *personalize*. In Part 4 of this book, we'll take a deep dive into how to personalize your process to better connect with the right customers in the right way, whether you're working on a handful of six- or seven-figure deals or tens of thousands of direct-to-consumer transactions worth a few dollars each.

E | Exceed expectations

The letter *E* in SUPER is all about exceeding expectations. In today's competitive environment, customers aren't just comparing you to the best product or service they've received from your competitors. They're comparing you to the best product or service they've received *anywhere.*

Exceeding client expectations isn't a nice-to-have—it's a must-have. In Part 5 of this book, we'll talk about intentional experience design, getting buy-in from your team, and how to recover when a customer's expectations aren't met.

R | Repeat

SUPER customer experience doesn't happen by accident. It happens when systems are designed, taught, implemented, and measured—again and again. By the end of this book, you'll be equipped with the tools you need to wow your customers, whether you're a part-time solopreneur, a customer service rep, or the leader of a billion-dollar brand.

◀◀ SUPERQUICK! REWIND ◀◀

Customer experience is not a department—it's a philosophy that must be embraced by every member of an organization. When executed correctly, it becomes your most powerful competitive advantage. This is encapsulated in the SUPER Model:

S. Start with your story.
U. Understand your customer's story.
P. Personalize.
E. Exceed expectations.
R. Repeat.

Inside each of us is
a natural-born storyteller,
waiting to be released.

ROBIN MOORE

PART 2

START WITH YOUR STORY

5

Who Are You

· · · · · · · · · · · · · · · · ·

Find out who you are and do it on purpose.
DOLLY PARTON

T HE EASIER it is for a customer to get something similar to whatever it is you're offering, the better your experience must be. Otherwise, you'll be seen as a commodity and lose on price, or speed, or any other variable customers can compare directly across your competitors.

So, don't lead with features and benefits. Instead, create a differentiated experience right off the bat with an impactful story. Once a customer has an emotional point of connection, your competitors won't stand a chance.

MyMetalBusinessCard.com is a website that sells—wait for it—metal business cards. When new customers request samples from the site, they receive an email like this from founder Craig Martyn:

Hi Brittany,

It's Craig here. I'm the president and founder of My Metal Business Card.

I've been a model train geek since I was born. In fact, I was so deep into it that I founded a model train manufacturing company. . . when I was fifteen. Yes, really.

Running that model train manufacturing business required LOTS of learning about manufacturing—both in the U.S. and overseas. And with teenager obsessiveness, I quickly became very knowledgeable on processes ranging from injection molding to wire forming and one specific process that would change my career: chemical etching.

I was lost in some deep thoughts about that production process when I landed on the idea of metal business cards. You see, the chemical etching process can also be used to produce stunning metal business cards—that's the one connection between my model train manufacturing business and My Metal Business Card.

After the idea struck, I researched the market and found dated websites and design style, high prices, poor quality, etc. Yet I could see the product had so much potential to allow companies to WOW their clients, land new gigs for professionals and bands, and stand out from the crowd.

My years in the model train business taught me a lot about running rigorous manufacturing, quality assurance, responsiveness to customer needs, and helpful and attentive customer support.

I knew I could provide a superior product and service, so I set out to produce the HIGHEST quality metal business cards in the world.

Fast forward a few years, and MyMetalBusinessCard.com has become the leader in the metal business card space. We've sold metal cards to Facebook, Tesla, Uber, Ford, and thousands of other companies, big and small. Over 10 MILLION cards, in fact.

We have over 3,500 5-star reviews across a range of review sites. And I won't be satisfied before we get one more from YOU.

I want you to make a lasting impression with your prospective and existing clients and partners. Please be in touch and let me and my team know what you need to stand out in your business—we're here to make you a star among your customers.

Sincerely,
CRAIG MARTYN

There are a few standout things about this email. First, Craig introduces himself as a *person*, not just a CEO. We can imagine him as a fifteen-year-old kid trying to figure out overseas manufacturing. Next, he does a nice job of setting up the problem (poor quality, high prices, bad websites, and so on) that led him to *switch tracks* (I couldn't resist) and get into the business of business cards.

Craig juxtaposes the weaknesses of his competitors with an expert-level humblebrag: his team has more than 3,500 5-star reviews and has worked with superstar brands. Then, he brings it home: "I won't be satisfied before we get one more from YOU."

Boom.

There are lots of competitors in the metal business card space, but after getting Craig's email—and then receiving the free samples his team sends—customers don't want to roll the dice with someone else. Why choose an also-ran when you can work with the category leader? A compelling, memorable story will set you apart from the competition.

Here It Goes

Storytelling is all about positioning: the space we take up in our customers' minds. If you aren't clear on where that space should be, they won't be, either. Your story helps define your position by answering questions about what you're the best at and why that matters.

Where do you want to live in your prospects' and customers' minds? When do you want them to think about you, and why?

Answering these questions will help you begin to unlock one of the most powerful tools each of us possesses: a story that will be valued, remembered, and *shared*.

Our brains are hardwired to remember and react to stories. This evolutionary truth has played a role in oral histories that have been passed down over millennia. It can also help savvy marketers and salespeople close deals by expertly setting the stage for their customers.

One of the first questions I get when I say "start with your story" is this: "Are you talking about the *brand* story or the individual employees' stories?"

The answer? Both. Because much like the Chicago Bulls and Michael Jordan, they are intrinsically linked. One is a key character in the story of the other, just as each employee is a character in the story of your brand as it plays out in real time.

In Chapter 20 we'll talk more about crafting stories for the *brand* to tell. If you're a founder or solopreneur, there will be a lot of overlap in those stories. However, it's important for *each* employee to be able to explain how, and *why*, they got to the position they're in. It's tantamount to being able to show that they care—because if your employees are apathetic, your customers will be, too. One of the best ways to "connect the dots" between a brand and its employees is with employee origin stories.

I'm a proponent of every employee at a company building their personal brand. Not only does it help the individual, it also helps the company. Think about it: people buy from people. Why wouldn't you want *your* people to be perceived as the very best? Origin stories are a powerful way to accomplish this goal.

IF YOUR

EMPLOYEES

★ ★ ★ ★ ARE ★ ★ ★ ★

APATHETIC

★ ★ ★ ★ YOUR ★ ★ ★ ★

CUSTOMERS

WILL BE, TOO

Everyday Superhero

Think about your favorite superhero. They have a compelling origin story, right? Whether it's Peter Parker getting bitten by a radioactive spider while living with his aunt and uncle or a young Wonder Woman training on the island of Themyscira, there are defining life events that pushed that character to become who they are. Events that propelled otherwise ordinary people onto an extraordinary path.

Your origin story is no different. If you think back on your life, there's a good chance you can draw a line from your childhood to what you're doing now. You may have to take a bit of creative license, but all of life's best stories sometimes blur the edges.

An origin story provides context and purpose to the position you're in and helps your customers understand how you got to where you are, and why you are uniquely positioned to serve them.

Motivational speaker Larry Winget once said, "Discover your uniqueness and learn to exploit it in the service of others, and you are guaranteed success, happiness, and prosperity." Your origin story is your uniqueness. It helps you stand out, but it also makes you *uncopiable.* Once you've nailed it—and figured out how to connect it to your customers—you'll be unstoppable. (Don't worry; we'll talk about connecting your story to your customers' stories a few chapters from now.)

If you're thinking, "What I'm doing right now is just a job. It's not a calling," then please reserve your judgment for a few more pages. I promise that you (and everyone on your team) can create a compelling personal origin story that potential customers will remember.

I Wanna Talk About Me

Here are three origin stories about yours truly. Each is true, but a casual observer might assume they're describing three different people. You can take creative license to connect the dots between the meaningful moments of your past and where you're at now. The finished product will be a memorable story that helps people say, "I get it!" and "That's who I want to work with," whether you're the longtime leader or the new kid on the block.

POSITION: *Advertising agency executive*
KEY ROLE: *Winning and keeping brand clients for the agency*
AUDIENCE: *Brand managers and C-level executives*

I wanted to work in advertising before I even knew what "advertising" meant. While my cousins were annoyed by commercials during our favorite Saturday morning TV shows, I was mesmerized by them: I loved the cadence of the jingles, the poetry of the slogans, and the intricate stories that could be told in thirty or sixty short seconds. I can still hear every word of the "My Buddy" and "Kid Sister" jingles and see the Kool-Aid Man busting through brick walls.

My parents hated taking me to the grocery store because I would insist they buy the brands whose ads resonated with me. I'm not just talking about shunning the cereals that didn't have memorable mascots—I would make impassioned, mid-aisle scenes about everything from cold cuts to condiments based on store signage or ads I'd seen, pleading: "After all, it's Butterball!"

It wasn't just ads, either: I was—and still am—obsessed with product packaging. My mom still tells the story of how she came into the bathroom to check on me when I was about seven years old and had been in the tub for a long time. The problem? I was stuck in a seemingly endless loop of washing my hair because of the words "rinse and repeat" printed on the back of the new Pantene bottle. Every time I rinsed, I repeated.

When I look back, it's not surprising that my obsession led me to a career in advertising. That love sparked my decision to attain my master's degree in marketing with a focus on shopper marketing and consumer behavior. I wanted to be part of the elite club of people whose job it was to make consumers fall in love with products through clever, carefully designed campaigns.

Cute story, right? Hopefully, it evokes images of a precocious little girl whose love of advertising took her from rural Oklahoma to Madison Avenue. Let's talk about a few of the intentional decisions I made when crafting this story.

First, it references specific brands and products, like Pantene, Butterball, and Kool-Aid. This is important because my target audience at the time was focused on building their own brands and each reference was an opportunity to connect with them. Hopefully, the audience would have their own fond memory of one of the brands mentioned in this story and, on a subconscious level, would feel closer to me because of our shared experiences.

Second, the story includes a memorable, self-deprecating anecdote. The depiction of me as a confused, very literal seven-year-old is a story people will remember. When choosing key snapshots to include in your origin story, consider humorous ones that allow the listener to get a quick laugh at your expense. Don't ever make a joke at the expense of your prospects or customers, though, or you might come across as arrogant or mean. (Pro tip: making fun of your target audience is never a good strategy!)

Third, I get to tout my credentials—a master's in marketing with a focus on consumer behavior—in a way that doesn't seem forced. Because many of the brand managers whose business I was trying to win had MBAs, I knew dropping a quick mention of my degree was relevant. Think about what credentials matter to your target audience and find a way to weave them in organically.

Last, I make references to family members because my target audience was largely made up of women trying to sell products to other women shopping for their households. These story snapshots were designed to connect and endear me to them.

Did I ever tell that story word for word? No, but mapping it out helped me draw a direct line from my past to my current role and shaped the way I introduced myself to my peers and prospects. It will do the same for you and your employees. Writing, and then internalizing, that story enabled me to pull out those details strategically over the course of conversations almost automatically and introduce opportunities for commonalities—read: connecting *my* story with *their* story—more quickly.

Likewise, this origin story was useful as I pitched clients to win new business—as were the other dozen or so vignettes I plucked from my past to recite as appropriate to help illustrate why I was the perfect partner for whatever business opportunity I was vying to win. (We'll talk more about building a collection of supporting stories in the next chapter.) The purpose of *any* story is to connect with the audience.

I wasn't a founder at the advertising agency. I wasn't even in the C-suite. It didn't matter; I still needed a strong origin story because *every* employee represents the company. My prospects and customers wanted to get to know who they would be working with on their account. Your customers are no different. Whether an origin story is being conveyed in an instant (like a hometown printed on a cashier's

THE PURPOSE
OF
ANY STORY
★ ★ ★ ★ ★ IS TO ★ ★ ★ ★ ★
CONNECT
WITH THE
AUDIENCE

name tag) or over coffee, sharing details from your life leads to deeper-felt connection.

I quit my job at the advertising agency after about eighteen months. It turns out it wasn't as much fun as I imagined it to be when I was a kid! So, I launched an entertainment startup.

Startup founders spend a lot of time pitching their businesses and, by extension, themselves. Whether they are looking for customers, investors, press coverage, employees, or vendors, their storytelling is an everyday affair. Here's how I shifted my origin story to fit the new role I found myself in.

POSITION: *Startup founder*
KEY ROLE: *Everything, including winning artist and brand clients*
AUDIENCE: *Artist managers and record label executives*

My career in the entertainment industry began with the most entry-level gig possible: a radio station mascot.

When I was sixteen, I spent an afternoon at my local radio station "job shadowing" for a school assignment. I was captivated by the energy of the station: the glass control-room booths with energetic disc jockeys, the seemingly endless array of phone lines blinking with listener requests, and CDs and cassette decks as far as the eye could see. I begged the station's promotions manager for a job—any job—and was thrilled when she said, "You look like you're about the right size for our mascot suit."

I said yes on the spot. I couldn't believe it: I was going to be Sting the Bee, B98's beloved mascot! I started turning up at every furniture store grand opening, rodeo, state fair, and car-dealership sale within a fifty-mile radius. I didn't think life could get any better. Not only did I get into every event for free (albeit while wearing a bee suit in 100 degree temperatures), but the station paid me! I was making $10 an hour, which felt like an enormous sum to do a job I would've happily paid the station to let me do.

A few months later, toward the end of my junior year, I got the kind of lucky break that I thought only happened in 1980s teen comedies. I had the good fortune of having the last name of Jones. The first movie adaptation of the uber-popular *Bridget Jones's Diary* was about to premiere. Our station promotions manager, Tammy, said, "Everyone's talking about that Bridget Jones movie. We've got a Brittany Jones. We should do something and call it Brittany Jones's Diary."

Remember: to this point, exactly no one outside of Roland High School knew that the station had "a Brittany Jones." It wasn't like I was on-air talent. I wasn't even on the station's website. I wore the bee suit.

With all the bravado of a teenager with nothing to lose, I said, "Well, you're always talking about driving traffic to the station website. What if I interview all the bands that come to town, and we can call that my diary?"

Without missing a beat, my boss said, "That's perfect. It's like that other movie people are talking about, *Almost Famous*. Let's do it. Make a list of the bands you want to meet, and we'll coordinate all the details with the record labels."

And, just like that, it became my job to hang out with rockstars and brag about it on the internet. For the next three years, and through a series of happy coincidences (like "blogging" becoming a word people knew), I had adventures that dwarfed anything I could've dreamed up in my mind.

This early discovery that someone could get paid for such a "job" ruined any chances of me ever getting a quote, unquote *real* job. From that moment forward, a career in the entertainment industry was the only option.

I interned at every record label that would have me. I toured with unsigned bands, doing everything in my power to help each one land their "big break." And, through the course of it all, I became more and more obsessed with the concept of superfandom—which, after stints in the marketing department at two of the three major label groups, is what led me to where I'm at now.

I started the entertainment agency ZinePak (which later became The Superfan Company) as a continuation of what I've been doing since I was a teenager: telling meaningful stories that connect fans with the artists they love. I know what it feels like to love your favorite band more than anything. I harness that feeling to put fans first in *every* decision I help artist clients make.

Again, every word of this story is true, although I don't mention anything about the advertising memories I shared in the first story.

It's also not a complete snapshot of the entire timeline. I gloss over about a decade from the time I worked in radio to starting my company. But it's not a resume. It's not a list of product features and benefits, either. It's an origin story. The idea is to help people understand who you are and why you're where you're at by telling them how you got there.

I had several versions of my startup origin story, each designed to resonate with different audiences. The same might be true for your origin story (or stories). In 2019, when I sold most of my equity in The Superfan Company to focus on keynote speaking and writing full time, it was time for a new origin story. Here's what I came up with.

POSITION: *Keynote speaker*
KEY ROLE: *Winning mainstage speaking invitations*
AUDIENCE: *Meeting planners and corporate executives*

The first time I heard myself speak into a microphone was at my preschool graduation ceremony in 1988. I don't remember why I was chosen to address the audience that day, but I do remember seeing my parents, grandparents, cousins, and fifty adult strangers in the audience and thinking, "This is neat. I want to do this again."

When kindergarten started, I couldn't wait to begin auditioning for speaking parts in our school programs. I lobbied for every chance to be in front of a microphone. I practiced for hours in front of imaginary audiences, talking into the little red My First Sony microphone that I begged my parents to buy me for my sixth birthday.

Some of my proudest moments in high school were the speech competitions I won with my original oratories and delivering the valedictory speech at my high school's graduation, just like I'd done the last time I donned a cap and gown back in 1988.

A few of my college professors suggested I pursue a career in public speaking, but I never seriously considered it because I had my heart set on working for a record company. It took more than a decade—and dozens of speaking engagements at conferences and events for organizations including American Express and the United Nations—before I finally listened to the message the universe had been sending me.

I spent most of 2018 pulling double duty: running my entertainment startup and traveling across the country for speaking gigs with corporate clients. I hadn't planned it, but each speech I delivered led to several more invitations, and my calendar snowballed.

I ended that year exhausted but grateful and decided something had to give: I couldn't keep balancing what was becoming two full-time jobs with a toddler and two dogs at home. So, I sold much of my equity in my entertainment agency to focus on speaking full time.

I've never felt happier or more fulfilled. And—while this sounds crazy—every now and then when I walk off a stage in a hotel ballroom, I see my little five-year-old self, smiling up at me in her graduation garb, saying, "I told you! This is pretty neat. What took us so long to get back here?"

Again, it's a different framing of the exact same life to highlight what I'm doing now. Like the first two origin stories, everything in it is true: I can draw a direct parallel to what I'm doing/selling now all the way back to defining moments and events throughout my life. By highlighting them, I can help prospective customers feel like my career choice wasn't accidental; instead, it was somehow "meant to be." Most people like to be inspired, and many like to think we're all part of some bigger plan. Tap into those two near-universal emotions when you frame your story.

That last origin story is also designed to answer a frequently asked question—*Why did I decide to leave my startup when things were going so successfully?*—before people have the chance to ask it. And, again, there's a bit of a humblebrag when I share the truth that I was getting lots of referrals (often called "spin business" in the speaking world) when I first began appearing onstage.

Writing my origin stories helped me to think more critically about how I could convey important information to my prospects and customers to connect with them more quickly. The exercise will have the same impact for you.

(What's the Story), Morning Glory?

Once when I was teaching a workshop on origin stories for a group of insurance professionals, a man told me that he'd been inspired to start a career in insurance because of a pivotal moment in his childhood: a flood in his small hometown destroyed the general store his family had owned and operated for generations.

It was the only time he saw his grandfather or father cry. In one stormy night, the family lost everything. And, because they didn't have flood insurance, they were left to rebuild with very little help. They hadn't even realized the store was in a flood zone, and no one had ever talked to them about the need for a separate flood insurance policy.

He'd been drawn to insurance to help ensure that the tragedy that struck his family wouldn't be repeated. The craziest part? He'd never told a customer or prospect his story before. "I just never thought much about it," he said. "I didn't realize how relevant it was. But, you're right, customers would probably like to hear that story."

Of course they would. That origin story catapults his job from "profession" to "purpose." It takes him from a commodity seller to a category of one. Your origin story will do the same, regardless of the role you're playing in your organization.

I hope your mental wheels have been turning during this chapter. Are there connections you're noticing now in your own life that you never thought about before? Perfect, because an origin story is just the beginning. In the next chapter, we'll dive into some of the other must-haves in your storytelling repertoire.

◀◀ **SUPERQUICK! REWIND** ◀◀

Your origin story provides context and purpose to the position you're in now and helps customers understand why you're uniquely positioned to serve them. Here are some tips for crafting it:

- Know your audience, and customize your story accordingly.

- Be specific about details and fill in any necessary gaps.

- A little self-deprecation never hurts.

- Tout your credentials.

- Tap into universal emotions—make the prospect believe that your career path was meant to be and that you're both part of something bigger.

6

My List

. . . .

Great stories happen to those who can tell them.

IRA GLASS

F YOU'RE EVER in Nashville, try to go to a songwriters' round. There are several of them every night, from famed venues like the Bluebird Cafe to dive bars and hotel lounges, where songwriters take turns playing acoustic renditions of their songs and sharing the stories behind them.

Country music has always been about storytelling. Because many songs aren't written by the artists who make them famous, songwriters' rounds are a fascinating look into the process. One of the paradoxes of songwriting that I've learned from attending countless shows over the years is this: the more personal a lyric is, the more universal it will be in its appeal.

It seems strange at first, right? Wouldn't a more general sentiment connect with more people? No. The magic is in the details. Our brains think in pictures, and the more details we hear, the more we create images in our heads. However, the cool thing is that our brains create images specific to *us*.

When you hear someone sing about their hometown, you think about your hometown. When they sing about their job, you think about your job.

Even if the details they sing about don't match your experience at all—let's say the "first love" an artist is singing about took place one summer at a beach in the '80s, but your first big romance was in Arkansas in 2001—your brain makes the connection. You may be overcome with nostalgia as their words cause you to recall feelings from your past.

The more specific the details in the stories you share, the more personable—and memorable—you'll be. People will feel like they know you better and open up more.

This Is Me

What makes *you* the very best choice for customers to do business with?

If you can't answer that question confidently and definitively, how can you expect a prospect or customer to be able to? More directly, if they can't readily discern why you're the best, what's the logical conclusion? That you might not be the best. Otherwise, the answer would be obvious.

The higher the price point of the item you're selling, the more important becomes the truism that people don't buy from companies, they buy from *people*. The best businesspeople know that the customer is buying *them* as much as they're buying the product or the service. It's about creating an experience. Building a relationship. Curating a physical or emotional space that leaves the customer saying, "That was wonderful. I can't wait for next time."

According to research by Salesforce, 80 percent of customers said the experience a company provides matters as much as the product or service it's selling. That experience begins with the story every employee is conveying, both verbally and nonverbally.

The Way

Storytelling has become something of a buzzword in business over the past couple of decades. More and more executives are starting to embrace what humans have intuitively known since the beginning of our existence—that a great *story* can inspire and mobilize people more quickly and more effectively than any amount of data, facts, or logic.

There are many popular, helpful models for crafting stories. At BrittanyHodak.com/SUPER you'll find a list of recommended resources to help hone your message, depending on your circumstance and objectives. As a shortcut, make sure every story (and I'm using the term loosely, as some might argue that what follows are anecdotes or vignettes) you tell passes the "Who, What, Why" test. If it does, you're on the right track.

Who

Who is this story about? You are the "who" in any first-person story you tell, including your origin story. However, as you build out the rest of the stories in your Story Setlist (which you'll learn about next), it should be apparent who all the characters in the story are.

Listeners need anchors. Presenting a character that we can *connect* to in some way combats apathy and piques our interest by giving us a reason to care. Even if you're only briefly setting up the character ("Back when I was just your typical suburban latchkey kid...”), it’s important that your audience knows *who* the story is about.

What

“What happens?” In Hollywood, a short synopsis of a movie is called a logline. It’s a bite-sized overview of the “what.” The action. The major plot point. The event that creates a demonstrable change and makes the story worth telling. What happens? Without this element, the story will be boring at best, and apathy-inducing at worst. What’s the moment in your story that makes things *no longer like they were before*?

Why

Finally, there is the “why.” *Why* does the “what” matter? This is the most important component of all, because without a compelling “why,” you’ll never overcome customer apathy.

Remember: superfans are created at the intersection of your story and every customer’s story. If they don’t care about—or worse, don’t understand—your story, it’s game over.

Who—What—Why. Admittedly, this mini framework is an overly simplified take on what countless people have elevated into an art form, but it’s a helpful rule of thumb to begin thinking about the stories in your life that merit sharing. It’s also useful for making sure you don’t accidentally leave any gaps.

What’s Going On

Our brains aren’t just hardwired to react to stories—they’re designed to fill information gaps where they exist, too. When a customer

★ ★ ★ SUPERFANS ★ ★ ★
ARE CREATED
— AT THE —
INTERSECTION
OF
YOUR STORY
— AND EVERY —
CUSTOMER'S
★ STORY ★

doesn't have all the information they need to make a decision about you or your brand, one of a few things happens.

The first possibility is that apathy sets in. They don't care enough to care, and they move on with their life. Perhaps they look for another solution or decide the problem isn't something that needs solving just yet. Either way, they don't progress past awareness to action.

Another option? Your prospects fill in the gaps in the story themselves. When this happens, sometimes they get the details right and sometimes they don't.

Once, when my son Kadoh was three and pretending to feed breakfast to his superhero toys, I heard him ask his Batman action figure how he was enjoying his blood. I asked him why he was serving blood to Batman, and he said, "Because Batman is a vampire." You see, he explained, vampires wear capes, go out at night, and hang out with bats. And so does Batman. Therefore, Batman is a vampire.

Even when you do everything you can to make sure your customers get all the details right, they can still put it all together in a way you didn't intend. Sometimes, you'll show them Batman and they'll see a vampire. You may never know they got it wrong, and they might not, either.

Uncertainty gaps can create enough cognitive dissonance that customers simply don't buy from you at all because they can't figure out which decision is the right one. Or maybe they'll use your company as a starting point to find a competitor. They may even be savage enough to google "[your name] vs" and let the search engine's autofill suggestions do the rest.

But don't fear! A tremendous story helps fight off potential apathy before it even stands a chance. Next, you'll learn a system for always having a list of memorable anecdotes at your disposal to share strategically throughout your customer's journey.

Ready, Set, Go!

Setlists are the lists musicians create each night to order the songs they're going to play. Copies of these lists are often taped on the stage floor in front of each band member so everyone knows which song is coming next.

Maybe you've been lucky enough to take home a copy of the setlist after a memorable show at some point in your life. Or maybe you've visited the website Setlist.fm to relive one of your favorite concerts. If you haven't, check it out . . . it's a wild trip down memory lane!

Bands who make a living playing bar gigs have setlists, too. But, unlike with arena acts, the setlists of bar bands are much more fluid. After all, they don't have to worry about being in sync with pyrotechnics, costume changes, or other carefully choreographed elements. They've got a rough idea of the songs they'll be playing, but the order isn't set in stone. They read the room, react in real time, or maybe even pass around a tip jar for requests.

We're going to take a bar-band approach to building something for you that I call a Story Setlist: a go-to list of stories you can pull from as needed to start a conversation or keep one going. Just as you need to follow up a debut single with an amazing first album, you've got to continue to set yourself apart with standout stories, no matter how good your origin story is.

Now, if you're thinking, "I don't want to be the jerk with the rehearsed stories who is always talking about themselves," first: I applaud your self-awareness. You should be proud. Second, I want to remind you that the first pillar of the SUPER Model—S: start with your story—does not mean *lead* with your story. I would never try to turn you into that person at the improv comedy event with too many suggestions. You will deploy these stories strategically and only when the timing is right.

Having a go-to list of stories will help you forge deeper relationships more quickly, because stories accelerate the path to connection. Telling the right story to the right person at the right time can take an otherwise apathetic prospect or customer from awareness to advocacy almost immediately. Stories can elevate you from a somewhat interchangeable commodity provider to a *real* person with a unique and interesting perspective in someone's mind in a matter of moments.

The sky's the limit in how you weave these details into the fabric of your business. You can include your employees' hometowns on their name tags or invite them to put their favorite quote at the bottom of their email signatures. Your crew could wear their favorite team's jersey to work on the weekend or mention their favorite treat to everyone who goes through the checkout lane. These small actions help humanize everyone on your team and increase the odds that your customer will leave the experience remembering a friendly conversation sparked by a common connection. And, just like recording artists, we're going to separate our stories into two buckets: originals and covers.

The originals

Your originals are unique stories about yourself and your life. These are the things you've done, experienced, accomplished, and so on. When trying to decide if a story is worthy of adding to your setlist, ask yourself the following three questions:

1   Is it memorable? Just like an artist doesn't want to put "meh" songs on their album, you don't want filler stories in your setlist. If a story isn't likely to be remembered by the person you share it with, don't add it. Stories with familiar themes or characters are likely to be remembered because the listener will have a frame of reference for what you're talking about.

2   Is it remarkable? The best stories are unique and striking. If there's a story in your arsenal that regularly earns a response like, "I've never met anyone who [*your awesome thing here*]," it belongs on your setlist. Think of the last time you played "two truths and a lie." What were the wildest truths you came up with? What's your funniest story from high school? What do friends say about you when they introduce you to others? These anecdotes may belong on your Story Setlist.

3   Does it evoke emotion? Good stories make the listener *feel* some-thing! If there's a hook in your story that reminds the listener of something in their own lives, that's a bonus. Many relationships have formed over a shared sense of nostalgia or common emotion. When I described seeing Matchbox 20 in the Enterlude, did your mind flash back to your own first concert experience?

The exercise of gathering your originals should be fun. Get creative! Do you love *Friends*? Then start every one of your stories with "The one with..." in homage to the episode titles in that series. Is travel your jam? Name 'em after airport codes. Whatever you do, just make them memorable so you don't forget to tell them.

Pretend you're a reality TV show producer trying to get someone hooked on your story. Where would you start? What details would you share?

From social media to speed dating, once you're looking at a set-list with the most fascinating details about your life, you'll find lots of opportunities to share them. And, once you begin deploying these stories, you'll quickly find they make you more memorable.

One of my favorite examples is from my friend and record company executive Lloyd Hummel. Lloyd loves coffee—especially Starbucks coffee. What Lloyd doesn't love is when the Starbucks baristas mis-spell his name.

★ STORIES ★

ACCELERATE

★ THE PATH TO ★

CONNECTION

What began as a couple of funny one-off posts several years ago showing things like "Lowd" and "Loid" scrawled across coffee cups soon became a long-running bit. For *years*, Lloyd has frequently shared artistic shots of his name—mostly misspelled—on coffee cups. Loyed, Load, Lloid . . . you name it, and he's probably posted it. I'm talking dozens and dozens and dozens of unique butcherings of his name.

I never tire of seeing Lloyd's java pics in my social feeds. They always get high engagement from Lloyd's connections because they're relatable. Just about everyone can connect with having their name misspelled somewhere, even if they aren't coffee drinkers. Or maybe they've worked where they had to write customers' names and can relate to the stress of it.

Here's the magic part. I don't just think about Lloyd when he posts funny pictures of his coffee cups. I think of Lloyd *every time* I see a Starbucks cup. Sometimes I think of Lloyd when my own name is misspelled, even if it's not on a coffee order. We haven't worked on a project together in a decade, but he crosses my mind almost every week. You know the last time I thought of several of the other people I worked with during the same timeframe? The last time I worked with them.

That's the power of positioning—and one of the reasons your Story Setlist is so valuable. When you share a detail or story about yourself that is unique, people begin to associate *you* with *it*. Then, they don't just think of you when they're thinking about whatever it is that you sell. They think about you on random Sunday mornings or on a Thursday after work. They wonder what you're up to and think to themselves, "I should send them an email." Then, when a colleague asks for a referral, they're much more likely to think of you because it's only been a few days since they thought of you instead of eleven months.

One of the stories on my setlist is about being a radio station mascot. It's fun, it's memorable, and it ties in well with the "superfan" concept, since so many sports teams, brands, and entertainment properties have both mascots *and* superfans.

When I'm at a sporting event or a convention and I see a mascot, I almost always stop for a picture. Posting the photos online gives me a fun chance to talk a bit about whatever fandom I've just experienced while also serving as a subtle reminder to the people who know about my mascot background that I got my start in a bee suit.

What happens, over time, is that I begin to hold positioning in people's minds when they see mascots—almost subconsciously at first, and then more overtly. I know this because almost every week someone will text, DM, or email me a photo of them with a mascot. *Saw this and thought of you!* the messages often read.

BINGO. *They thought of me.* They were out living their lives, doing something completely unrelated to me, and I crossed their mind. Which means I'm top of mind . . . exactly where I need to be to generate repeat business, referrals, and relationships that last. Mission accomplished.

Because our brains think in images, not in words, you can get creative with the methods you use to be "sticky" in the minds of your customers and prospects so that they think about you when they're out and about, too. (Bar setlists are also sticky . . . but it's usually from the beer and the wings.)

We've all done interesting things and have stories that are note-worthy. Two of my friends, Kelly and Andrew, renew their vows every year on their anniversary at the park where they were married. Because of this, I think of them every time I hear about someone renewing their vows.

Crystal Washington, a futurist and professional speaker, loves candy corn, that ever-polarizing Halloween staple. I can't stand the stuff, but every time I see the waxy, tri-colored sugar triangles, I think about Crystal and smile.

Jason Duff has spent the past decade buying and restoring historic buildings in Bellefontaine, Ohio. Whenever I see a story about someone giving new life to an old building, I think of Jason and wonder what he's up to.

You've already got a mascot or candy-corn example in your life. What memorable details are likely to be a hit with your audience? For more ideas and prompts (and a downloadable template that looks so rock and roll that you might want to frame it!), visit BrittanyHodak .com/SUPER.

The covers

Just like musicians learn to play other bands' songs before they write their own, you can hone your storytelling chops by calling on some "covers": stories you've heard or seen elsewhere.

Did you just hear a fascinating story on a podcast that you can't wait to share? Maybe you binge-watched a new TV show and have zero chill about it. Or perhaps you heard a joke on the radio that made you belly-laugh. When things resonate with you, there's a good chance they'll resonate with others. Make a mental note of your favorite parts (or, better yet, *write them down!*) and you'll be ready to rock with these stories in no time. You know that fun friend who always has interesting things to share? That's about to be you.

Born This Way

If you're worried that you've only got one or two setlist-worthy stories, I assure you that's not the case. Even the most introverted among us can craft stories that will alter the thoughts, actions, and lives of others. You've just got to believe that you can.

Allow me to drift into motivational territory for just a moment. If you don't believe that you *deserve* superfans, it's going to be very hard to create them.

You have a uniqueness that no one else on this planet has. By connecting your story with the stories of the people whose paths you cross, you can change the world.

The stories we tell ourselves are among the most important stories in our lives. Especially the stories we tell ourselves *about* ourselves. The thoughts we have shape our actions and our realities. The stakes are much higher than just glass-half-full or glass-half-empty.

Jon Acuff is one of my favorite authors. His book *Soundtracks* is about the stories we tell ourselves. More precisely, it's about how to challenge the repetitive negative self-talk so many of us are plagued by—talk he refers to as "soundtracks" playing over and over in our heads—with *new* soundtracks, aka positive talk. In other words, you can transform overthinking from a super problem into a superpower.

Even if personal development books aren't your jam, this one is worth a read. Or, even better, a listen. The audiobook is fantastic because Jon is hilarious. Jon proposes this simple framework for overcoming negative thoughts: "Retire. Replace. Repeat."

1   Retire your broken soundtracks (stories and beliefs that aren't true or are no longer serving you).

2   Replace them with new ones.

3   Repeat those new ones until they're as automatic as the old ones.

If you struggle with overthinking, or if you find yourself regularly telling yourself that your dreams or goals are impossible because you're not *something* enough to reach them, add *Soundtracks* to your reading list. Then, build out a setlist that showcases the most remarkable things about you and your business.

◀◀ **SUPERQUICK! REWIND** ◀◀

A standout story can inspire and mobilize people more quickly and more effectively than any amount of data, facts, or logic. Curating a setlist of go-to stories that you can pull from as needed helps you build rapport with prospects and customers. You can use covers or originals that are memorable, remarkable, or that evoke emotion.

People don't care how much you know until they know how much you care.

THEODORE ROOSEVELT

PART 3

UNDERSTAND YOUR CUSTOMER'S STORY

7

The STORY of Us

. . . .

Empathy is a quality of character
that can change the world.

BARACK OBAMA

MY HUSBAND isn't allowed to set up usernames anymore.

In 2009, about a year after we were married, we moved from a tiny studio apartment on the Upper East Side of Manhattan to a slightly-less-tiny one-bedroom apartment. We loved everything about the new building except for one thing: it wasn't yet outfitted with Verizon's Fios service, so our only option for internet was Time Warner Cable.

Like many utility providers, Time Warner didn't have the best reputation for service or customer care. When I called to set an appointment to turn on our service, I was told the waiting period was ten days—a virtual eternity to go without internet and TV.

Jeff and I flipped a coin to decide who would stay home from work on our appointed day, since the service window was something like "8 a.m. to 4 p.m., unless we end up not coming. If that happens, don't call us, we'll call you." When I got home from work the evening of the install, Jeff told me the technicians had arrived around 1 p.m., stayed for a couple of hours, and left. Our TV and internet worked, so I didn't ask questions or give it another thought.

Until three days later.

The internet stopped working and we couldn't figure out why. We exhausted all of our technical know-how (meaning I unplugged the modem twice and pushed some unmarked, blinking buttons) before deciding it was time to call the dreaded Time Warner Cable customer support line. Jeff argued that, since he had been the one to wait around for service all day, I had to make the call. That seemed fair, so I dialed the number and settled in for my estimated fifty-six-minute wait time.

When I was finally connected to a rep, he asked me to provide my Time Warner username. I said we'd just received our service a few days ago and hadn't set one up yet. He replied, "You definitely have a username. You have to set it up while the technicians are there."

I called over to my husband and he said, "Oh, yeah. Our username is timewarnersucks."

That's right. Not only had my husband chosen "timewarnersucks" as our username, now I had to say it *out loud* to a rep from the company whose help we were depending on. I sheepishly recited it, and after a brief pause he said, "Okay. Please verify your password."

I was mortified when my husband shared it with me: *reallySucks!* I wanted to disappear into a puddle as I said something like, "Uh, our password is, um, well, my husband set it up, and it's . . . really sucks exclamation point, with a capital *S* at the beginning of the word sucks, and it was all my husband, and I'm so sorry!"

The agent was silent for a few seconds. Then he said, "You said you just got your service hooked up three days ago? I'm surprised that username was still available. I would've bet money it was already taken."

In an instant, he turned around what was an *incredibly* awkward situation for me into something we could both laugh about. He would've been justified in being a jerk. Instead, he led with empathy. He wasn't just helpful; he was kind and funny, too. That call completely changed the way I thought about the brand. No longer was the first thing that came to my mind when I thought about the company its long wait times or intermittent outages—it was a helpful agent who showed me more grace than I deserved.

It Takes Two

Empathy and authority are an unbeatable pair. Too many times, when talking to a customer, salespeople and service representatives don't take the time to really listen. They lead with authority at the expense of empathy, often because they're confident they already know what the customer will say and what the solution should be. They are so anxious to share what they *know* that they forget to show the customer that they *care*.

Ian Koniak, a sales trainer and speaker, uses the phrase "commission breath" to describe the phenomenon that happens when a salesperson is so eager to sell or share something that the customer can smell desperation. They just! can't! wait! for the customer to stop talking so they can hear their own voice again. Newsflash: that's not an effective way to sell!

In fact, it's not a very effective way to do much of anything. Whether you're in sales, marketing, public relations, customer service, product development, legal, or any other department, empathy is a critical skill, and it should always precede authority.

The quickest way to get someone to care about you and the things you care about is to demonstrate that you care about them and the things they care about. One of my favorite lessons about understanding others comes from Oprah Winfrey. On the final episode of her long-running syndicated talk show in May 2011, she said this:

> I've talked to nearly 30,000 people on this show, and all 30,000 had one thing in common: they all wanted validation.
>
> … Every single person you will ever meet shares that common desire. They want to know: "Do you see me? Do you hear me? Does what I say mean anything to you?"
>
> … Validate them. "I see you. I hear you. And what you say matters to me."

Customers don't want to feel like just another number or another order. Whether they're spending a few dollars with your business or a few billion, they want to feel seen, heard, and valued. Put simply, they want to feel like they matter as much to *you* as you matter to them.

Superfandom is a two-way street. If you want your customers to love you, you've got to love them back. Period. And, it's really hard to love someone you don't even know. That's why understanding your customer or prospective customer's STORY is key, and the second pillar of the SUPER Model framework.

I Think I Understand

Did you catch the caps on STORY in that last sentence? Much like a hotline bling, those uppercase letters can only mean one thing: I'm about to hit you with another acronym. That's right: an acronym within an acronym. It's kind of like the movie *Inception*. Or, if you prefer, it's like the turducken of customer experience. Choose whichever you like best! Just try to remember this STORY (write it down if you have to), because it's going to help you accelerate your path to creating superfans.

In general, I'm not a fan of customer personas, also called customer avatars. I think they're too broad and, in many cases, give marketers and salespeople an excuse for ignoring entire segments of the population because they've been led to believe they're not "in the demo."

Perhaps you saw the meme circulating online some time back that juxtaposed then-Prince Charles with Ozzy Osbourne. It noted that both were wealthy, prominent, twice-married males who were born in the U.K. in 1948 and reside in castles. The side by side was, as the meme went, an example of why demographics alone aren't sufficient to create buyer personas on.

While including psychographic characteristics undoubtedly makes for stronger profiles than demographic-only personas, they are still lacking. Instead, become clear on the customer STORY you're trying to understand. It's a system you can use to help guide discovery conversations and build trust and rapport and, ultimately, figure out if your thing is the right fit for someone. Here's how it breaks down.

S | Struggles

One of the quickest ways to get a prospect to care about whatever you're selling is by showcasing that you understand their problem, perhaps even better than they do.

What's the problem your customer is trying to solve? What struggles are they facing every day? Even if you *think* you know the answer, be sure to ask questions to get a deeper understanding of what they're struggling with.

Even before you have a chance to ask about struggles, do your research. It's never been easier to get real-time information about an individual or a business. Are you trying to sell a solution to a company? Make sure you've been a *customer*—or at least witnessed as much of the customer journey as possible. Visit a physical retail store. Call the customer service number and see what the experience is like. Spend some time on their website and social media pages. If it's a publicly traded company or a nonprofit, check out their annual reports. Do a Google News search. See what customers are saying on Tripadvisor or Yelp or the Better Business Bureau website, and see what employees are saying on Glassdoor.

There's nothing worse than a salesperson with an "I solve one problem, and I bet you have it!" approach who has made no attempt to understand their prospect's unique position, objectives, or struggles, or a customer support rep who assumes everyone is calling to resolve the same issue.

T | Transformation

Think back to your favorite late-night infomercial from back in the day.

Whatever the enthusiastic narrator was selling—ShamWows, Bumpits, George Foreman Grills, it doesn't matter—there was always a moment when the black-and-white "before" video would zoom in on a distressed person saying, "There's got to be a better way!" Then, the Miracle Product™ appeared and, just like that, everything was different. Life was forever changed. Easier. Happier. Better!

What is the transformation your customer is looking for? What about their life isn't working right now, and what changes will come when your Miracle Product™ enters the mix? Because *real* change extends far beyond the surface problems others may see, emotional transformations are where superfans are made.

If your product helps shave half an hour off a customer's workday, what is the transformation? Is it added productivity? No. It's the gift of *time* and the freedom to do anything with it. Maybe it's getting to have dinner at home with the family. Maybe it's going to a hockey game.

The transformation may have nothing to do with your solution on the surface, but it's got everything to do with how connections are made.

The same is true in customer service. When I called Time Warner Cable about my internet and TV being down, it wasn't about the $2 or whatever I was paying that day for service—it was about what I was missing *because of* the outage. The transformation I wanted was simple: being able to watch live TV again. Thankfully, this was before Trevor Noah took over as host of *The Daily Show* (the one program I *never* miss!), so an ill-timed outage didn't rise to the level of Category Five emergency.

You immediately increase your odds of success when you sell the transformation, not the product. How can you make someone's life better? What's going to move them from that low-def, black-and-white freeze-frame of exasperation to the high-def, Technicolor life of happiness?

O | Options

The quickest way to lose a customer is by assuming they have no other options. There is always another option . . . even if that option is to throw an epic party or invest money in crypto instead of buying your thing.

Recently, Jeff and I were in the market for new garage doors. I don't know if you've ever had to buy garage doors. If so, my condolences. If not, trust me when I say that it's even less fun than it sounds.

We went to the website of one of the big-box home improvement stores and followed its instructions to come to the store to meet with an "expert." We printed out the details of the exact doors we wanted, left the kids with a sitter, and headed to the store.

More than two painstaking hours later, after several instances of the expert putting information into the store's computer incorrectly, he told us a third-party vendor would come to our house in a few days to confirm our details. The good news? He assured us we would have new garage doors in about ten weeks. We paid a deposit and left.

"What a waste of time that was," my husband remarked on our drive home. I agreed, saying, "There is no reason we shouldn't have been able to do that online in fifteen minutes."

When the third-party vendor arrived, we learned that several of the details the store employee had provided to us were incorrect. It was going to be twenty weeks, best-case scenario, but probably more like twenty-four. But the good news, according to the vendor, was that we would be getting a refund of several hundred dollars because the width of our doors was less than reflected on the initial invoice. Bad for backing out of the garage (my poor, scratched side mirrors!), but good for garage-door cost savings, apparently. We'd just need to go back to the store one last time for a quick trip to finalize the details.

The second quick trip turned out to be *another* two hours. And, instead of the refund we were told to expect, the employee quoted us several hundred dollars *more* for the smaller doors. He couldn't explain why his price was different from what the vendor quoted, but he assured us that it didn't matter because we'd encounter the same prices (and wait times) regardless of where we went. He did not think he was in jeopardy of losing the $7,500 deposit we'd already put down on the doors. He was wrong.

We canceled our order, and, instead of spending thousands of dollars on beautiful new carriage house–style garage doors with windows and hardware accents, I paid a repairman $270 to fix our broken garage doors. Then, I spent $30 on Amazon to buy magnetic accents that look nearly identical to the windows and hardware detailing I liked so much on our would-be doors. The transformation was eye-popping—and it cost $300 instead of $12,000. Don't make the mistake of thinking your prospect or customer's only options are your direct competitors. There are *always* other options.

YOUR CUSTOMER ALWAYS HAS OTHER OPTIONS

Examples of enterprising customers are everywhere. When a chiropractor told writer/editor Emily Schultz she was going to need an expensive, drawn-out treatment program for her aching back, she instead spent a fraction of that estimated cost on a new mattress and bed frame. Her problem was solved faster and much less expensively than if she'd gone ahead with the chiropractic treatment plan, and she didn't have to schedule all those trips to the office. Your option is never the only one.

R | Reservations

One of the best ways to overcome customer objections is to raise them before they do. When possible, reframe what could be perceived as a negative in a positive light. If you expect cost to be an issue, for example, proactively talk about the return on investment or the cost savings over time.

When you're talking to a customer, whether you're trying to land your first deal with them or your fiftieth, don't skip past their reservations. You don't have to use the word "reservations"—instead, you can say things like, "Is there anything keeping you from saying 'yes' today?" or, "Is there anything about the solution we've discussed that you don't feel excellent about?"

It's always better to uncover reservations before the sale than after. The last thing you want to do is take a sell-it-and-walk-away attitude. An unhappy customer (or even one suffering from a small dose of buyer's remorse) might cost you a dozen future customers. Every customer is an influencer. Every deal can shape a hundred more. Be a resource for your customers, answer all of their "what if?" questions, and help guide them into the best fit for them—even if that fit is at another company or service provider.

Y | You

Only after you're clear on your potential customer's struggles, trans-formations, options, and reservations can you know if you're the right fit for their specific need.

If you are, wonderful! If not—and I cannot stress this enough—*say so.* Tell them. Never take money from someone you don't think will be a good fit in the long run, even if it's 3 p.m. on the last day of the month and the deal is the only thing standing between you and hitting your quota.

I can't begin to count the number of five-figure speaking engage-ments I've turned down in the past few years for people who asked me to speak on areas outside my core expertise.

Would the money have been nice? Yes. But I wasn't the right fit for the client, so it wouldn't have been the right move in the long run. I'm sure I could've done a good job, and they would've likely been happy with the outcome, but I'm not going for "good" and "happy." I want every engagement to be *amazing* and for my clients to be *thrilled,* because referrals and repeat customers are the lifeblood of every successful business, including mine. My customers become partners. We work together again and again.

When I'm not sure if I'm exactly the right fit, I say so. Then, I make recommendations for people I've met over the years who are likely a better match and offer to make the introduction.

It's a win for the prospect because, instead of a good fit, they get an amazing fit. It's a win for whomever I refer because I know they're getting a client who is exactly in their lane. And it's a win for me because I get the karma points for teeing it up.

Putting customers first is always the right choice in the long run, even if it means pointing them in another direction. And you'll see the ROI in amazing, often unpredictable ways. Someone who went through the customer journey but didn't buy from you based on your

TARGET SUPERFAN #1

Superfan Name _____

Partner ☐ OR Customer ☐

Age _____ Location _____

Profession _____

Family Status _____

Fun Facts _____

Struggles

Transformation

Options

Reservations

You

honest feedback is going to bring you a lot more business over the next decade than a customer who wishes they'd never signed on the dotted line in the first place.

If It Makes You Happy

I mentioned at the start of this chapter that I'm not a huge fan of creating customer personas or avatars. However, I also recognize that many (many, many!) organizations still use them. If yours is one of them, you can use the customer STORY framework to create as many avatars as you want. You can even give them silly, alliterative names.

Hop over to BrittanyHodak.com/SUPER to download, fill in, and print customer personas to your heart's content. Just don't forget that *people* take priority over personas, and we're not living in a *WandaVision* world where we can bend every prospect's story to fit a predetermined narrative for the sake of simplicity.

◀◀ SUPERQUICK! REWIND ◀◀

Empathy and authority are the one-two punch that can't be beat. Use them in equal parts to show your customers how much you care so that they'll care how much you know.

To connect your story with every customer's story, you've got to understand the struggles that led them to this point, the transformation they're hoping to undergo, the options in the customer's mind that are competing with whatever you're offering, any reservations they have about moving forward, and whether you are the best solution to their problem.

8

Read My Mind

. . . .

*Most of the successful people I've known
are the ones who do more listening than talking.*
BERNARD BARUCH

W HEN YOU don't fully understand your customer's STORY, you can be doomed before you even get started. I learned this lesson the hard way.

I was in Los Angeles to film an episode of the television show *Shark Tank* for my first startup and had what I thought was an "aha!" moment completely unrelated to the business I was there to promote. The production company gave show contestants per diems in an envelope each day to cover meals, as is the standard for union productions.

At the time, the union per diem was $63—far more than I spent on my meals. By the end of the production week, I had amassed a few hundred dollars of unspent per diems. As I was leaving my hotel, I saw a homeless gentleman and gave him some cash for food. I thought about how many people in need could be fed for $63 per day.

Then, I thought about the tens of thousands of high-net-worth individuals who regularly get per diems as part of their contracts. Professional athletes. Actors. Business executives. Surely, the wealthiest of these individuals—all of whom had more than the means to buy their own meals—could spare those per diems. If there was an easy way to turn that relative pocket change into meals for people in need, would they do it? My gut said they would.

I learned that professional baseball players, who spend much of the year on the road, were paid more than $10,000 in contractual per diems each season. I was also shocked to discover that food insecurity—unreliable access to enough affordable, nutritious food—affects 1 in 6 Americans, including 1 in 5 children.

I was already running a full-time business (for which I had just accepted a deal from two TV Sharks for nearly three quarters of a million dollars), so this shouldn't have been my focus, and yet I couldn't stop thinking about the idea. I shared it with my cousin Jennifer at Christmastime, and she couldn't quit thinking about it, either. We decided to join forces and bring the idea to life. It seemed perfect on its face: reallocating money meant for food from those who didn't need it to those who did. It had a Robin Hood–esque quality.

My cousin and I incorporated a 501(c)3 called Per Diems Against Poverty and started making phone calls. One of my first calls was to Feeding America to see if they'd like to partner on the initiative. They said yes and generously offered to help with any necessary support. It felt like a major victory and a sign that our charity was going to help change the world.

Jennifer and I decided that 100 percent of *every* dollar donated by individuals would go directly to Feeding America. That meant I'd be covering our overhead until we were up and running enough to get corporate sponsorships. My plan was to ask businesses to match the per diems they were paying to their C-level execs to cover administrative costs in phase two of our charity. I thought things would get off the ground quickly, so I didn't mind covering costs to get us started.

I thought the next logical step was to get some press, so I began pitching the concept. Within a month, I had a feature in *Forbes* and a TEDx about food insecurity lined up. Soon, CBS *This Morning* did a feature story on us that aired nationwide.

Jennifer and I toured food banks and food pantries across the country, immersing ourselves in the tremendous need for food rescue and reallocation in our country. I went to bed and woke up thinking about families in communities like mine all over America who don't know where their next meal is coming from. I learned everything I could about per diems. I started reaching out to everyone I knew in industries where their usage was commonplace.

I was not expecting the obstacles we encountered. Professional sports leagues were afraid that allowing players to participate would go against union rules. Players told us they appreciated the intent, but they'd rather make donations to their own communities rather than to our organization. Others said that, because they'd experienced food insecurity themselves, they were investing every penny they made during their careers to make sure no one in their own family would ever go hungry again.

We found equally unanticipated challenges in other verticals. What we hadn't considered for Hollywood, for example, is that while the *superstars* are making seven or eight figures per film, most of the cast and crew aren't. Many of them don't know when they'll get their next job, so donating per diems is out of the question. We learned that a common practice in Hollywood is for stars to give their so-called "envelope money" to crew members. The same is true in the live music industry.

About a year into our endeavor, although we'd signed up a handful of athletes and other partners, it became apparent that—as perfect as this idea had seemed on paper—it just wasn't going to work. After spending thousands of dollars on startup, administrative, and travel costs, plus countless hours trying to bring this idea to fruition, I finally admitted to myself that my contribution to the fight against food insecurity wouldn't be through this charity.

My cousin and I made the classic mistake that too many excited entrepreneurs and businesspeople make: we decided our solution was *right* before talking to the prospects whose support we would need as customers—or, in this case, donors.

We were so caught up in our story and the problem we wanted to solve that we didn't listen to the customer's story. Had we taken the time to do so, we would've learned that many professional athletes had struggled (S) with food insecurity and poverty in their pasts and, because they didn't know how long their careers would last, were investing every dollar they collected, including per diems. (One player told me, "They don't say 'The NFL stands for Not For Long' for nothing. If I get injured, this all goes away tomorrow.")

While we thought the transformation (T) of reallocating per diems to local communities was a great idea, it turns out it wasn't the right transformation for the right audience at the right time. There were several other options (O) for giving to worthy causes—some players and actors have their own foundations, while others prefer to give directly to charities they've supported for years.

One reservation (R) we encountered again and again was that people didn't understand what purpose we were serving. Many appreciated our efforts but asked, "If you're giving 100 percent of the donations to Feeding America, why shouldn't I just give to Feeding America directly?" It was a fair question . . . one we didn't think through well enough before jumping in headfirst to solve a problem.

That leads into the final consideration (Y): Were Jennifer and I the *right* people to solve this problem? We certainly thought we

— DON'T DECIDE —

YOUR SOLUTION

IS THE

★ RIGHT ONE ★

BEFORE TALKING TO

YOUR CUSTOMERS

were, but, as I've alluded to, it quickly became clear that we didn't know nearly as much about the space as we thought we did.

Don't decide your solution is the right one before talking to your customers. Don't try to read their minds, either, despite the title I chose for this chapter (from the Killers, aka the greatest band in the world—fight me!). Just make an effort to understand their STORY by practicing a critical skill called active listening.

Listen Up

I started interviewing recording artists when I was seventeen. In the two decades since I've had the honor of speaking with some of the biggest stars on the planet. From red carpets to TV shows, podcasts to print magazines, I've found that active listening is the key to getting an epic interview.

I'm sharing the process here, because the same tips will work for customers, both pre- and post-sale. Celebrities: they're just like us! There are five steps to active listening, and you can practice them in any conversation . . . no famous friends required.

1. Listen attentively

The first step, unsurprisingly, is to listen with your full attention— not, like, 95 percent of your focus while you're thinking about that trip to the grocery store later or trying to mentally place exactly why the name of the person you're talking to sounds so familiar. Give the person your undivided attention in the way four-year-olds give their undivided attention to a costumed Marvel character. Doing so will immediately place you in a small category.

As Stephen Covey said, "Most people do not listen with the intent to understand; they listen with the intent to reply." Understanding your customer's story is critical to creating superfans, so listen like your job depends on it. (Spoiler alert: it does!)

2. Repeat what you hear

This is the step that separates active listening from passive listening. As soon as the person you're speaking with has finished talking, repeat back what you heard. This helps ensure there is no misunderstanding.

In sales, this step can sound like: "I heard you say that your number-one priority is reducing employee turnover by 20 percent year over year and that a solution needs to be presented to your board of directors by March 31 for approval." A customer service agent might say, "In the eighteen hours since you last saw your credit card, you've been notified of four large charges you did not make."

Repeating their words reassures the other person that you're giving them your entire attention and demonstrates that you're detail-oriented in a "show, don't tell" kind of way.

3. Ensure you understand

Step three is as simple as asking, "Is that correct?" after your summary. Don't skip this step! Never assume that you're regurgitating the information correctly and put the onus on the other person to interrupt with clarification. Instead, immediately after you repeat what you've heard, ask, "Is that correct?" or "Do I have that right?"

One of two things will happen at this point: either the other person will confirm you have internalized their request correctly or they will offer clarification or correction. Sometimes, just hearing what they said repeated back to them can make a person realize that they didn't relay their request exactly right. This step helps uncover would-be issues or misunderstandings before they become *real* problems later down the line.

4. Ask a relevant follow-up question

The fourth step is to ask a relevant follow-up question (if needed) and then repeat steps one through four again until you have all the information you need.

This sequence speaks directly to Oprah Winfrey's wisdom in the previous chapter: everyone is looking for validation. There is no better way to offer validation than to actively listen. "I see you. I hear you. And what you say matters to me."

One of my pet peeves is interviewers who don't practice active listening. Maybe you've watched or read an interview with your favorite star and thought, "How did the host not ask a relevant follow-up question there?" Some interviewers are so intent on getting through every question on their list that they miss the opportunity to ask about something that's much more interesting.

Celebrities can tell the difference between someone who watched their new movie or listened to their album and someone who's just showing up because they're the reporter on duty that night. Customers can tell, too. Bring the same enthusiasm and curiosity to your professional conversations that you would give your favorite star on the red carpet and you'll get all the information you need and then some.

5. Retain and relay the information

The fifth and final step is to retain and relay the information provided to you. You may be capturing information during the conversation (taking notes, using an audio recording app, filling out a form, or similar), or you may not write anything down until the end of the exchange. Either way, make sure you're capturing everything you need for you and anyone else on your team who will need the information to further the client's requests.

This is an example of where customer relationship management (CRM) software comes into play in a big way. Even if some detail doesn't seem important now (for example, a client mentioned that his wife is going to Cancún on a girls' trip next month), you may want to add it to the Notes section of your CRM. That way, you'll be able to follow up the next time the two of you talk. When the fields in your CRM are customized with active listening prompts in mind, recording the information becomes simple and intuitive.

Active listening will improve communication with your friends, spouse, kids, and acquaintances, not just your colleagues and clients. Practice it in your conversations and it will become second nature in no time.

Listen to What the Man Said

In recent years, many organizations have added chief customer officers (CCOs) and chief experience officers (CXOs) to their executive teams to increase the customer centricity of their enterprises. These organizations quickly find out that there is no magic wand an executive can wave to turn the tide of an organization's culture. Customer centricity isn't something that can just be dictated by the C-suite—it's got to be instilled, enabled, and executed at each level of the organization.

Every employee is the most important ambassador of the company. Every interaction is the one with the potential to shape the company's reputation for the next decade. As if that isn't challenging enough, we've already established that every customer is an influencer. Every voice matters and deserves to be heard.

Enter VoC. In case you googled that, don't worry, I'm not talking about volatile organic compounds, which sound super scary. VoC is

EVERY
★ EMPLOYEE ★
IS IN THE
EXPERIENCE
DEPARTMENT

shorthand for Voice of the Customer. The term encompasses all of the ways you can gather feedback, both structured and unstructured, from customers, individually and at scale.

Those methods include feedback you ask for, like surveys, focus groups, product reviews, and interviews—and feedback that you might not ask for, including unsolicited emails, social media comments, blog responses, and so on. Some of the voices are delivered directly to your company (perhaps a call to your customer service center, a DM to your Twitter help account, or a text message to an account rep) and others are shared more openly (reviews, social media posts, and the dreaded comments section).

Although the customer isn't always right (see Chapter 13) and not every suggestion is a helpful one, listening to customers is critically important. It's free market research, right there for the taking. Understanding your customer's perspective (aka STORY) will make every member of your team more customer centric and more empathic.

It's never been easier to glean information about what customers do and don't want. People are creating and sharing more content online every day than the totality of information businesses and professionals have had access to for about 99 percent of recorded history.

Social listening (paying attention to relevant conversations happening on social sites and forums, often with the use of a program to monitor specific hashtags and keywords) and search monitoring (looking for those conversations on blogs and websites) aren't nice-to-haves: they're mission-critical for every business that exists today, whether it's got six employees or 600,000. You absolutely must know what customers are saying about your brand, your employees, your products, and your competitors.

From a macro standpoint, VoC can improve your products, your processes, and your customer journeys. But from a micro standpoint,

VoC can improve *individual* outcomes for customers and turn them into superfans.

For VoC, especially social listening, to be effective, it needs to happen in real time. If you wait until the end of the week to have or find those conversations, they're already over. Customers have moved on. Show people you care by actively monitoring their questions and comments and addressing them immediately.

Do You Feel Like We Do

Someone once asked me, "How diverse does our executive team really need to be?" My response was, "Only as diverse as you want your customer base to be."

Representation matters, and one of the reasons diversity is such an important part of customer experience is because no person is going to have the background to represent all people. The more you have in common with the people helping you make decisions, the more likely you are to miss something that might be glaringly obvious to another audience.

I didn't realize the importance of nursing rooms until I depended on them while out and about with my sons. I didn't know how much website accessibility mattered until I became friends with someone who's blind. I didn't give much thought to people fasting during Ramadan until a Muslim client gently reminded me she couldn't meet for lunch or coffee for a few weeks.

We all bring our own biases, backgrounds, and blind spots into our decision making, no matter how much we might try not to. No matter how well you think you know your customer, your greatest learning will come from the things they tell you.

I should've done more homework before I decided to start a charity in an area I didn't know much about. I learned a ton about the problem before jumping in, but not nearly enough about the audience for whom the success of the organization would depend on. That's why there are so many jaw-droppingly stupid products and ad campaigns that make it to market—sometimes even from *huge* companies!—only to be quickly lambasted by the masses.

Seek out prospects, customers, and employees who represent as many backgrounds, beliefs, and experiences as possible. Then, do more active listening than talking. The voices of your customers and your employees are the most important ones in the world, and they can save you from embarrassing, expensive, and tone-deaf faux pas.

◀◀ SUPERQUICK! REWIND ◀◀

It's imperative to understand what customers are saying about you, your employees, your products, and your competitors. Active listening improves the quality of your information. Its steps are as follows:

1   Listen attentively.
2   Repeat what you hear.
3   Ensure you understand.
4   Ask a relevant follow-up question. Repeat as needed.
5   Retain and relay the information.

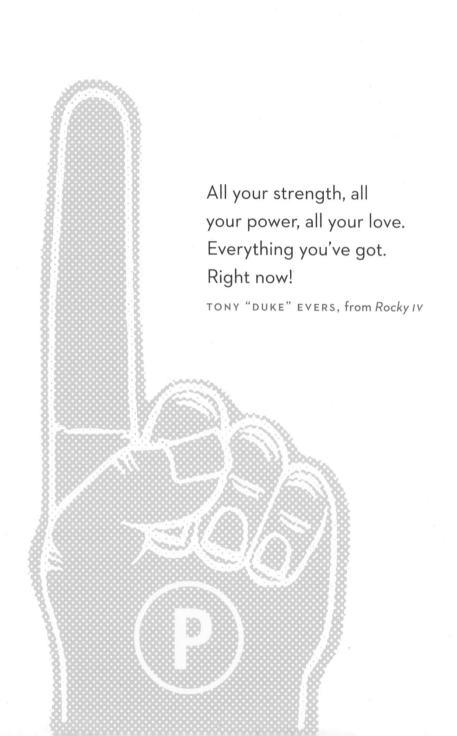

All your strength, all
your power, all your love.
Everything you've got.
Right now!

TONY "DUKE" EVERS, from *Rocky IV*

PERSONALIZE

I Want You to Want Me

. . . .

Customer service should not be a department.
It should be the entire company.

TONY HSIEH

MAYBE YOU'RE the kind of person who likes inspirational quotes in books. They're called epigraphs (my copy editor, Melissa, taught me that!), and I love them. That's why there are so many of them in this book.

The epigraph you read at the start of this part of the book is from *Rocky IV*. Why? For starters, it's a damn good quote. It's what Duke says to Rocky right before the final round of his bout with Ivan "If He Dies, He Dies" Drago.

Rocky IV is my favorite Rocky movie—and, yes, that includes the original and all the Creed movies. You might argue, "The original *Rocky* won three Oscars, including the Academy Award for Best Picture. Stallone created one of cinematic history's best characters in three days!"

You wouldn't be wrong. *Rocky* is an incredible film. But hear me out: *Rocky IV* has the best soundtrack of all the films by far, and the storyline is a masterclass in the perfect movie at the perfect time: Russia versus U.S. at the height of the Cold War? Epic. And, without that bit of inspirational dialog from Duke, maybe Rocky wouldn't have been able to finish the fight in Moscow on that cold Christmas day, rightfully avenging the death of Apollo Creed and winning the respect and love of those Russian fans. Plus, it felt fitting to use a quote from *Rocky IV* for Part 4 of a book about fandom, since (if you didn't pick up on it already) I'm something of a superfan of the franchise.

We've covered the first two pillars of the SUPER Model. S is start with your story, and U is understand your customer's story. I hope you can recite in your sleep by now that superfans are created at the intersection of your story and every customer's story. Now, we're at the part where those two worlds collide. The third pillar of the SUPER Model is P, personalize. Just like Rocky, it packs a major punch—especially when you put all your strength, power, and love behind it.

Kickstart My Heart

Several years ago, I was working on a campaign with Mötley Crüe legend Nikki Sixx. The video production dates kept changing because we were waiting on our retail partner to approve the scripts. When we finally got sign-off, the only time to film was during the band's Crüe Fest stop in Pennsylvania.

The problem? It fell during the weekend my brother Brandon and his daughter Hailey were visiting New York City for the first time. Hailey was turning six and had been looking forward to the visit for months. There was no one else I could send to the shoot in my absence, but, since my brother is a big Mötley Crüe fan, he said, "Let's all go to the festival—it will be fun!"

Management had generously hooked us up with all-access passes, so I took my niece backstage to grab some catering. She was trying to wrap her mind around all the different chocolate cake options when Nikki Sixx walked into the tent.

He came up to the dessert table, bent down to her level and, with a friendly smile and a wave, said, "Hi! I'm Nikki." He noticed that Hailey was wearing a *High School Musical* shirt and began asking her questions about the movie. He told her that his daughter loved Ashley Tisdale. Then he said, "You look like you're six years old." It was a couple of days after her birthday, so her eyes lit up as she said, "How did you know?" He didn't miss a beat: "Because my last name is Sixx. Did you know that? I can' always tell when someone is six!"

The three of us sat down and talked for a bit as my niece sampled all the different sweets. Nikki had no idea who we were (I eventually told him I was there to film the commercials)—he just saw an opportunity to make a guest feel welcomed and did so in a very personalized fashion.

Hailey returned to Arkansas raving to her friends about Nikki Sixx not because of his fame, but because he held his own in a conversation filled with topics that mattered to her: the Disney Channel, Hannah Montana, and the hierarchy of ice cream flavors.

Every conversation presents the opportunity to make the person you're talking to feel like the most important person in the world. Personalizing your approach shows every customer they are important enough to merit your undivided attention and creativity. They'll appreciate it and remember, even if you're not rock royalty.

Technology has made it so simple to use personalization that it's becoming an expectation for every customer. According to McKinsey & Company, 71 percent of consumers expect companies to deliver personalized interactions. Even more compelling? Three out of four customers get frustrated when it doesn't happen.

Every week, I look forward to receiving my personalized Progress Report from Fitbit. The company has come a long way from its humble beginnings selling Bluetooth pedometers. Now, its weekly email recaps information about my sleep, resting heart rate, exercise goals, and much more.

Fitbit knows that the information I care about is *my* information. By connecting their story ("A world of health and fitness in your hands") to my story ("Perfect! I care about my health and fitness"), they've conditioned me to look forward to opening their email every week, and have turned me into a loyal customer and advocate.

Another company whose weekly emails I never miss is Grammarly, a cloud-based proofreading app that checks things like spelling, punctuation, tone, and grammar. Every Monday afternoon when my Weekly Writing Update arrives, I open it to see how my stats stack up to those of other Grammarly users.

The email is always fun. The first words in my update this week say, "Check out the big vocabulary on you! You used more unique words than 99% of Grammarly users. Keep it up!"

An email that compliments me? Yes, please. It goes on to share my statistics on things like productivity and mastery and compares them to other users and even spotlights top mistakes (mine is missing commas in compound sentences . . . oops!).

My favorite part of the email is the Tone section. Since Grammarly's AI tool is always running on all my devices, it's able to detect the most common tones in my writing. For example, in the 106,540 words Grammarly checked for me last week, it scored me as 24 percent Friendly (up ten points from the previous week); 14 percent Appreciative; 14 percent Confident, and 11 percent Optimistic, among a few others. Do I need an AI robot telling me what tones I'm using? Of course not. I got by without it for three decades. But now that I'm hooked, I would miss it terribly if it didn't show up in my inbox every week.

How can you use personalization to create content and experiences your customers look forward to at every part of their journey? This isn't just a question for companies with mostly digital touchpoints, either. Technology has made it easier than ever to infuse your customer's story into your own. Direct mail is one example. Sports teams get very creative when sending marketing collateral. Whether it's a photograph of Michigan Stadium with what appears to be a customized message to the Hodaks on the stadium's scoreboard or a season ticket offer from the Nashville Predators with a player sporting a HODAK jersey (two recent examples from my own mailbox), personalization makes your customers and prospects pay attention.

I recently received a postcard from an allergy clinic near my house. It said, "More than 90% of people who are told they're allergic to penicillin are not."

I've been told since childhood that I'm allergic to penicillin, so the postcard caught my attention. I turned it over and read, "We can safely test you for a penicillin allergy. Penicillins are the safest, most effective antibiotics for many infections. Most people outgrow a penicillin allergy. To schedule your allergy test, call us today."

I scheduled an appointment for an allergy test, and guess what? I'm not allergic to penicillin after all—woo-hoo!

If I had received a postcard that said, "Call us. We do allergy tests," I would have ignored it and I'd still be trying to remember how to spell "penicillin" every time I fill out an intake form at a doctor's office.

Personalization is a powerful tool, even if you only have a couple of clues about your customer's story to work with. If it can make people voluntarily sign up for allergy tests, just imagine what it could do when deployed for your business.

One of the most compelling bodies of evidence for the power of personalization is the sheer number of songs that exist with women's first names in them. I bet you can name at least ten right now.

Seriously, just try it. Let's put twenty seconds on the clock, lightning-round style. Go!

There are a bunch of them, right? You know why? Because they *work*. Whether you're onstage at Madison Square Garden or your middle school gymnasium, singing a personal song for a *specific* girl is an extremely effective way to get her attention. Not *any* girl, *that* girl. She'll appreciate the attention . . . and so will your customers.

New Rules

What if you don't have access to a database of information on your customers and prospects? Follow three best practices. First, engineer every part of your customer's experience to be as simple as possible. Second, be as responsive as you can. Those two desires are pretty much universally shared. "If only it was more difficult and took longer to solve this problem," said no customer ever.

Beyond those two rules of thumb, the third rule—the one where the "personalize" pillar takes center stage—is to follow the advice of Dr. Tony Alessandra, coauthor of *The Platinum Rule*.

Many of us grew up with the Golden Rule, a playground staple that dates to at least 500 BCE. It is a tenet of most major religions and cultures. It advocates treating others as you want to be treated, or as you would want others to treat you. Alessandra's Platinum Rule takes the Golden Rule a step further: Don't treat others as *you* would want to be treated, but as *they* want to be treated.

Not everyone wants to be treated the same way. Others have different backgrounds, life experiences, personal situations, beliefs, preferences, access to technology, and so on, meaning their preferences may be different from yours.

TREAT OTHERS
★ ★ ★ **THE WAY** ★ ★ ★
THEY WANT
— TO BE —
★ **TREATED** ★

Customizing the "little" things, like asking your customers if they'd prefer to chat via phone, email, or text, shows that you're able to put their needs and preferences above your own and makes you appear easier to work with. Is it annoying having to send a paper statement to that one guy who refuses to go paperless? Of course it is. But it makes Jeff happy, so keep doing it as long as you can.

Unstoppable

I met Taylor Swift for the first time in the spring of 2007. I was working at a record company in Manhattan, and a friend invited me to fly to Nashville to attend the CMT Music Awards.

Taylor, whose self-titled debut album was released the previous October, was about to begin a record-setting awards season that would see her win several major awards on her meteoric rise to superstardom.

On this night in April, she received her very first televised award. Her song "Tim McGraw" took home the belt-buckle-shaped trophy for Breakthrough Video of the Year. I was sitting a couple of rows behind Taylor at the show. I don't think she anticipated winning the award, and her excitement was obvious.

At the after-party, I said hi and congratulated her on the award. She was with another artist I knew casually from interning at his label in college, so the three of us chatted for a while.

Taylor was seventeen and her debut album had just gone gold, which meant it had sold half a million copies. Much of her early success was attributed not just to her incredible talent and work ethic, but also to the way in which she reached out to her fans. She was very active on Myspace (one of the largest music-discovery sites on the internet at that time) and had a reputation for spending hours meeting her fans before and after shows.

She said something during our conversation that is burned into my memory: "I knew that if I wanted to get a gold record, I had to make half a million people care enough about me and my music to buy my album."

I've worked closely with hundreds of recording artists in my career and I've never heard anyone else distill so perfectly what it takes to build a legion of loyal followers. She cared about them—every single one of them—and soon, they cared about her too.

It's no accident that Taylor Swift is one of the biggest superstars on the planet. She's a brilliant songwriter and entertainer, but she's also one of the most innovative marketers in history. She knows that connecting *her* story with *her fans'* stories is key to lasting success. Every one of her album launches is a masterclass in how to connect with customers. From perfectly planned roll-out campaigns (listening parties, fan events, pop-up merch shops, and more) to the so-called "Easter egg" clues she loves sharing with her loyal listeners, no detail is too small to merit meticulous attention from Taylor.

Fans are the ones who stream music and sell out arenas. They're the ones who buy merchandise and watch documentaries. And, over the past fifteen years, Taylor has never missed an opportunity to make #Swifties, as her fan-army calls themselves, part of the action. She loves them, and they love her back.

If you want your customers to love you—not just like you, but love you to the point that they become advocates who are sending new customers your way—make sure they feel the love, too.

Be the One

. . . .

Once you've turned someone into a fan, you're their category of one. You're no longer part of some consideration set: you *are* the consideration set! Not only is your customer coming back, they're also likely telling their friends to check you out, too.

This is especially important for commodity providers—which, because of the way the world is changing, are many of us. Even if customers can get a nearly identical product or service elsewhere, once you create a superfan, you make price and competition irrelevant.

I'm a superfan of my exterminator, Scott. Despite my parents' best efforts, our house often had brown recluse spiders when I was growing up.

One night, when I was twelve years old, I was lying in bed, watching MTV. I went to brush a strand of hair off my neck and realized it was a spider, not my hair. I think that was the closest I've ever come to having a panic attack. My parents thought they were going to have to take me to the ER—not because I had been bitten (thank God), but because I couldn't calm down.

Brown recluse spiders are the creatures of nightmares. When they bite you, they cause a reaction in many people that makes the skin rot. As in, it turns gray and dies. Sort of like a zombie spider.

And, while the internet is split on the truth of this next part, I've always been told that whatever crazy venom they inject stays in your body and attracts other brown recluse spiders! *You become a literal spider magnet!* (I should note here that my mom read an early draft of this book and insisted I clarify that *she* didn't tell me this. She also believes my categorization of "frequent" spider infestations is overly dramatic. We agreed to disagree.)

One of the best things about living in New York City is that there are no brown recluse spiders there: the ground gets too cold in the wintertime. When my husband and I decided to move from Manhattan to Tennessee, I went into Google overdrive, binge-reading horrifying local news stories of people living in and around Nashville whose homes had become infested.

The first two pest control companies I called dismissed my concerns. "Don't worry, we rarely see more than a few brown recluses in that neighborhood. You don't have anything to worry about." You can imagine the cognitive dissonance I endured trying to reconcile "rarely" and "a few" with "don't worry."

The third company I called was Belle Meade Exterminating. The woman who answered the phone told me that she was also completely freaked out by brown recluse spiders and said that one of her teammates, Scott, would be happy to meet me to look at my house and put together a plan when I was in town for the inspection.

When I met Scott, he answered every question I had about the eight-legged assassins and told me exactly what he was going to do to make sure we had every line of defense. That was six years ago. Not only does Scott still come spray around my property for spiders every twelve weeks, he's also my go-to guy for all the other gross bugs that love Tennessee. Ticks. Mosquitos. Carpenter bees. You name it, and we've probably encountered it since we've been here. And Scott takes care of all of them for us.

I've spent thousands of dollars at Belle Meade in the past six years and have referred at least a dozen friends and acquaintances to them. Scott always responds when I text him pictures of weird bugs and ask how alarmed I should be. (The answer is usually "not at all.") On the rare occasion when a pest has been a potential cause for concern, he's at my house in a matter of hours to take care of it—and always with eco-friendly options, since he knows I'll be asking if it's safe for my kids and dogs. I ask every time. He never rolls his eyes . . . at least not in front of me.

Whether you're selling pest controls or paint or printers, you can absolutely make people care enough to become their category of one by providing superfan-level service. Care about them *first,* and then they'll care about you, and whatever your "thing" is. Connecting your story to your customer's story is a formula that works every time.

◄◄ SUPERQUICK! REWIND ◄◄

Personalization, at its core, is about treating everyone the way *they* want to be treated. By incorporating a customer's preferences into your interactions, you're not only making the experience more enjoyable, you're also showing them that they are important enough to merit individualized attention.

10

You Get What You Give

. . . .

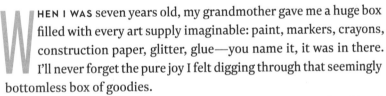

Since you get more joy out of giving joy to others, you should put a good deal of thought into the happiness you are able to give.

ELEANOR ROOSEVELT

WHEN I WAS seven years old, my grandmother gave me a huge box filled with every art supply imaginable: paint, markers, crayons, construction paper, glitter, glue—you name it, it was in there. I'll never forget the pure joy I felt digging through that seemingly bottomless box of goodies.

A decade later, for Valentine's Day my senior year, my boyfriend Christian bought me a giant teddy bear and decked it out with gifts and trinkets for me to discover one by one. At first, I thought it was just a cute teddy bear. When I looked closely, I found that Teddy was wearing a cute American Eagle jacket, a trendy necklace, bracelets, and one of those '90s-style backpack purses filled with more fun surprises, like nail polish and candy and a concert tee. It was one of the most fun gifts I'd ever received. All the items were my size and had been carefully curated and styled to surprise me.

What do both gifts have in common? They were creative, thoughtful, and centered on me. Put another way: they were *personal*. That's why I still remember every detail decades later, long after the markers dried up and the backpack purse went out of style. (Although, to be honest, we should really think about bringing those back!) They were more than gifts—they were the centerpieces of unforgettable experiences that made me feel like the most-loved person in the world.

I'm willing to bet the best gifts you've ever received were highly personalized, too. Yet, far too often, we settle for mass-produced mediocrity when it comes to corporate gift-giving.

Strategic generosity is one of the most powerful ways to create a "wow" experience for a customer and elevate the emotional closeness of a relationship. In fact, gifting checks every SUPER box: It's a way to connect your story (S) to each customer's story (U) in a personal way (P). When done correctly, it will exceed expectations (E), which is why you should repeat (R) the practice with all of your customers.

Not every professional works in an industry where they can leverage the power of gifts. For years, working closely with buyers and marketers at Walmart, I was unable to give gifts of any kind as they are a violation of Walmart's corporate policy rules. Even making charitable contributions in someone's honor was a big no-no.

Many people work in industries where gift-giving is highly regulated and cannot exceed a certain threshold (sometimes as low as $10). However, the reason generosity is so effective is that it shows the other person that you're thinking of them. It's not just about the gift (literal or figurative) or its cost; it's about the thought, effort, and time that went into it. At least it is when it's done correctly.

Even if you're operating with gifting restrictions, you can still use radical generosity to make an impression on your customers—and we'll talk more about that later.

Give a Little Bit

My friend John Ruhlin wrote the book on strategic gifting (Literally! It's called *Giftology*) and owns a corporate gifting agency called Giftology Group. He's proven time and time again that he's a master gift-giver.

At the beginning of 2021, I posted on Facebook asking for blender recommendations because I was tired of replacing cheap ones every couple of years. I complained that buying a high-end blender was more complicated than buying a car. Questions I encountered during my search included "Do you want a model that comes with Bluetooth?" which I am still unsure about the applications of, and "Do you want to buy a refurbished model?" (I did not.)

Several friends chimed in with recommendations. Two days later, a large box arrived: inside was a fancy new Vitamix blender. I had started a yearlong CXO engagement with Experience.com a couple of weeks earlier. The note on the gift-wrapped blender said, "Good luck *blending* your new role as a tech executive with mom life and keynote speaking! I'm rooting for you, as always. John."

Beyond the generous gift and kind note, John helped me by eliminating a decision that was dragging on way too long. He wasn't just giving me an appliance I would use frequently (and therefore think of him often), he was making my life easier with exactly the right gift at exactly the right time.

This is another example of where all the pillars of the SUPER Model framework come together to be more than the sum of their parts. John's blender gift was SUPER because:

- It aligned with his story, which is rooted in selfless generosity (S).
- It demonstrated that he was listening and understood a need (U).

- It was clearly personalized to connect at the right time (P).
- It was a surprise, thus exceeding non-existent expectations (E).
- Finally, John is always looking for these kinds of opportunities (R).

It doesn't take a $600 blender to make an impression on someone. The right gift at the right time is always impactful, regardless of its cost. I was thrilled to receive the blender, but I was also touched every time an employee or coworker noticed I worked through lunch and surprised me with a Dr Pepper and tacos at 3 p.m. Here are a few tips you can incorporate into your gifting repertoire to become a legendary gift-giver.

Think outside the office

I still remember the absolute *shock* I experienced the first time I saw my kindergarten teacher outside of school. I thought, "They let her leave school?" It had never entered my five-year-old brain that my teachers had a life beyond the orange-and-black brick walls of Roland Elementary.

Even though we're all grown-ups now, sometimes we forget that the prospects and customers we're trying so hard to create relationships with exist outside of their relationship with us. They've got interests, hobbies, and passions outside of work. You don't have to go with a gift that sits on or around a desk (or wherever it is that they do their work).

Make it a family affair

Want to know something else crazy I learned about those teachers who were allowed to leave school? Some of them had *families*! With spouses and kids and pets and everything! It was like they were living this other double life that I knew nothing about. Your customers have full lives, too. When was the last time you stopped to acknowledge the family members behind those contacts you value so much?

I'm talking about the daughter whose dad flies across the country once a quarter to meet with you or the son whose mom leaves at 4:30 every Thursday in the fall to get him to soccer practice. Maybe even the spouse who spent all his free time watching the kids so his wife could finish her book (thanks again, babe!).

Don't just show your appreciation to customers or prospects. Spread the love with the ones *they* love. It's not only good manners to acknowledge these supporting players, but also good business. While an ugly $39 golf shirt isn't likely to make an impression on a CEO, that same $39 on a LEGO set for his six-year-old is going to make him a hero at home.

A friend relayed a story about getting multiple six-figure referrals from a customer to whom he'd sent a $12 pack of tennis balls from Amazon for his daughter, along with a note wishing her good luck in a tournament that weekend. Talk about amazing ROI!

Make it unique

Even though gifts should be about the recipient, it's okay to connect your story to theirs in a meaningful way. In fact, it's more than okay because, as you absolutely know by now, superfans are created at the intersection of your story and every customer's story.

I once met a mortgage loan officer who said he loved his job because he was "one of the most important pieces of the puzzle for his borrowers." A few minutes later he told me he almost always attends closings in person, which means he's there "for the last piece of the puzzle."

I asked if he was a puzzle guy and he said, "I haven't always been, but I got really addicted to working puzzles with my wife during the first few months of COVID." I suggested he lean into his newfound affinity for puzzles and now, instead of the closing gifts he was accustomed to giving clients (a desk organizer with his company's logo), he instead creates a custom photo puzzle for each client that has a photo of the home they've just closed on. They cost him about $20 at the drugstore across the street from his office—he orders them via an app and they're ready to be picked up in an hour. The box showcases the photo (which always looks beautiful, because he pulls it directly from the listing), and is sent with a note thanking the client for "letting me be one of the pieces of your home-ownership puzzle."

Nearly every client he's gifted a custom puzzle to has been delighted. Many have shared photos of the completed puzzles on social media, often tagging him and offering effusive praise for anyone looking for a loan. Several have already made personal referrals. He's even seeing more business from his network of real estate partners, because so many of the delighted homeowners made a point to tell their realtors how much the closing gift meant to them.

When I asked how many clients he could remember who had posted photos of the desk organizer he used to send, he said, "Now that you mention it, none that I can recall." To him, it's about three clicks, a few bucks, and five minutes of total effort. To every client, it's a thoughtful, personalized gift they'll keep forever... and that will make them think of him every time they see it.

Mark the important dates

I'm a proponent of acknowledging birthdays and anniversaries if for no other reason than because, when you don't, your absence can be noticed. On my most recent birthday, I received more than a hundred marketing emails, texts, and social messages from brands and business associates. While I would never fault a person *or* a business for not acknowledging my birthday, it was interesting how a quick review of my inbox spotlighted some absentees.

I received both an email and a mobile push notification from Target, wishing me a happy birthday and offering me 5 percent off a shopping trip during my birthday month.

My first thought was, "Wow, that's nice of them." My next thought was, "Wait a minute . . . what about all those big-box stores I pay to shop at? Did they wish me a happy birthday?"

As it turns out, they did not. Despite paying more than $100 each for annual memberships for Walmart+, Sam's Club Plus, and Amazon Prime—and spending thousands of dollars annually at each retailer— none of them wished me a happy birthday. To borrow a line from *Full House*'s Stephanie Tanner, "How rude!"

A birthday note from a financial institution had the same effect when I realized that none of my *other* banks or credit card companies acknowledged the day. Don't give your competitors a chance to out- shine you by making it look like you care less by comparison.

Although plenty of brands and business associates were thinking of me on December 1, guess how many half-birthday wishes I got in June? Exactly two: one from my mom, and another from my husband. And, to be honest, I think they were both just humoring me. One of my friends read a draft of this book and told me, "American Eagle sends half-birthday coupons for 25 percent off!" I haven't shopped at American Eagle in years (don't tell anyone, but I think I've aged out of the demo), but I signed up for their mailing list in anticipation of the half-birthday hookup.

If you know your client's birthday, you know their half-birthday, too. Send them a quick card or email acknowledging the day. There's a good chance they may not even realize it's their half-birthday . . . which means you could make their day that much brighter. One year I

created custom half-birthday cards to send to all my favorite people—
they featured a caricature of Jon Bon Jovi and a parody poem about
being "halfway there."

Don't Do Me Like That

When you exceed expectations, you don't have to buy new leads—you
earn them organically, one enthusiastic advocate at a time. But there
are also some common gifting faux pas I've seen over and over, especially in organizations where customer-facing employees depend on
another department or outside vendor to fulfill gifts en masse. By
avoiding the mistakes that follow, you'll elevate your gifting game and
maximize the return on investment.

Don't put your name on it

If you were giving a friend a pair of fancy shoes for their birthday,
would you write your name on the sole so they would remember who
they were from? Of course not! Because it's a gift. It's about them,
not you.

While you would never do this in a personal setting, businesses
make this mistake constantly. The marketing department creates
swag, and then everyone at the company sends it out as "gifts" to
prospects and clients. It doesn't matter if it's an $80 hoodie or an
$80K Tesla. If you give someone something with your logo on it, it's
an ad, not a gift. You're asking them to advertise their connection to
your company, which makes it transactional: "Enjoy this while you
promote me for free!"

Don't get me wrong, swag has its place. Some companies create
amazing, highly coveted swag that their employees and customers
love. Just don't mistake it as a gift, because it's not.

IF IT HAS

YOUR LOGO

★ ★ ★ ★ ★ ON IT ★ ★ ★ ★ ★

IT'S AN AD

NOT A GIFT

Don't ignore 90 percent of the calendar

Don't only show gratitude in December. I once heard the word "Creasters" used to describe Christians who attend church services exactly twice a year: on Easter and Christmas. As in, "I'll have to get here an hour early next Sunday to get a parking spot because I'll be competing with all the Creasters."

Client mailboxes, like church pews, are more packed than usual during the holidays. Giving gifts between mid-November and mid-January isn't a strong strategy. There's a ton of competition and the gifts feel somewhat obligatory—just another component of the check-the-box marketing plan.

Showing appreciation should be a year-round activity. If you absolutely *must* send a gift during the holidays (although my preference is a heartfelt card), follow as many of the guidelines in this chapter as you can to help increase the odds of a memorable experience for the recipient. Otherwise, consider a less-crowded gifting occasion instead. Love your customers? Show them on Valentine's Day! Feel lucky to have them? St. Patrick's Day it is. Would life be scary without them? Tell 'em on Halloween, before your competitors all hit them up at Thanksgiving. You get the idea.

There are at least 360 non-crowded days of the year to make your customers (and employees!) feel special. You don't even have to use *real* holidays. There are endless hashtag holidays constantly cropping up for people who love #coffee, #pancakes, #pizza, and just about everything else under the sun. When in doubt, make up your own occasion. Or, celebrate #SuperfansDay every year on January 10, which is a totally real thing that I didn't make up just now to promote this book on its release date anniversary.

Don't expect anything in return

Never give a gift with expectations or conditions. That isn't a gift—it's a bribe. Not only is it bad form, it's also a good way to make yourself look like a jerk. If you can't give a gift without any expectations in return, don't give it.

And on the other side of that coin, never try to use a gift you've given in the past as leverage. Don't, for instance, say something like, "You know, the reason I got you the luxury box at the Cubs game for you and your brother is that you told me the deal was getting close. It's been six weeks—are we there yet?" Once a gift is given, it's been given, don't bring it up again. You don't get to hold on to the good-gift points for future credit, like coins in a Super Mario game.

One last "don't"

Last but not least, don't send anyone a gift that requires more than five minutes of assembly, unless it's a puzzle or a LEGO set or another gift where assembly is part of the fun. A gift that must be put together before it's capable of being enjoyed isn't a present—it's a project. The exception, of course, is coordinating the delivery and assembly for the recipient. If you can do that, proceed. If not, consider another gift.

Listen to Your Heart

Gift-giving is not the only way to practice radical generosity. There are endless possibilities to make people feel appreciated and valued. You can volunteer your time to important causes, make donations to beloved charities, create works of art, cook meals . . . the list goes on and on.

One way to be generous is sharing information that others may find helpful. You can recommend a book or a restaurant or an excursion that you think your customer or prospect will enjoy, based on what you know about them. This positions you as helpful while also giving you an excuse to reach out. It also reinforces the fact that you "get" them.

If you're unable to give actual gifts for any reason, be it regulatory or company policy or simply because you have no budget, you can still showcase your generous spirit and exceed your customers' expectations. You can make your audience feel seen, heard, and appreciated by sending a card, a nice email, or even a text. If you've got time to include relevant, thoughtfully curated information, whether it's a movie recommendation or a deep dive into a topic you know they care about, even better!

◀◀ SUPERQUICK! REWIND ◀◀

When leveraged correctly, strategic gifting is a wonderful way to build relationships and show your customers that you care about them.

Do:

- Get a gift that incorporates a customer's interests or hobbies outside of work.

- Consider gifts for family members so your customer gets to be the hero.

- Send thoughtful letters or emails to show your appreciation.

- Celebrate smaller holidays, even ones created by social media.

Don't:

- Put your company logo on a gift.

- Rely on the holidays as your only gifting opportunity.

- Use your gift as a bribe or expect anything in return.

- Give something that creates a lot of work for the recipient.

MODEL

THREE

PERSONALIZE

FOUR

EXCEED EXPECTATIONS

FIVE

REPEAT REPEAT

SUPER

THE ★★★★★★

ONE
START WITH YOUR STORY

TWO
UNDERSTAND YOUR CUSTOMER'S STORY

★★★★★★★★★★★

The key is to set realistic customer expectations, and then not to just meet them, but to exceed them—preferably in unexpected and helpful ways.

RICHARD BRANSON

EXCEED
EXPECTATIONS

11

All the Small Things

. . . .

*Great things are done by a series of
small things brought together.*
VINCENT VAN GOGH

I N A HUMOROUS collection of observations called *New Math*, New York–based author and artist Craig Damrauer summed up modern art in this equation: "MODERN ART = I COULD DO THAT + YEAH, BUT YOU DIDN'T."

Funny, right? Perhaps you've had a similar thought at some time in the past, walking through a gallery at MOMA or reading news out of Art Basel. Remember the banana duct-taped to the wall that sold for six figures? Bet you wish you'd tried that!

A slight tweak to Damrauer's equation is the perfect summation of both customer and employee experience: EXPERIENCE = I COULD DO THAT + YEAH, SO WHY DON'T YOU?

Everything that's in this book is, on the surface, simple. None of it is rocket science. Most of it isn't even expensive. And yet, that simplicity is deceptive. If it were *easy*, everyone would do it.

Every fast-food restaurant would have service like Chick-fil-A. Among hotel chains, the Ritz-Carlton would be the rule, not the

EXPERIENCE

═

I COULD DO THAT

+

YEAH, SO WHY ★∴ DON'T YOU? ∴★

exception. Every online shopping experience would be as seamless as Amazon's, from the one-click buying to the quick and predictable delivery. Visiting any theme park would be as magical as a day at Disneyland.

But, of course, that isn't the case. These fan favorites work tirelessly to ensure the customer experience is predictably and consistently excellent. Every member of their team knows exactly what is expected of them in every interaction. They don't just routinely meet their customers' expectations, they exceed them.

Embracing the SUPER Model will help your team differentiate itself and win lifelong customer advocates. Experience is everything, and everything is experience. That duality is, in a nutshell, the heart of what it means to be living in a time of an experience economy. Keep that in mind as we dive into the next pillar of our framework— E: exceed expectations.

Every interaction—before, during, and after each transaction— contributes to the totality of a customer's experience, and therefore what they remember and share. Your email signature is part of the experience. So is whether or not your customers can track their orders on your website. The header image on your LinkedIn profile.

Even the outgoing message on your answering service. The vet I used to take my dogs to at some point switched her answering service to a cringeworthy default message. Every time I called her office, a recorded voice instructed me to:

> Press one for directions and hours. Press two for prescription refills. Press three for cremation and euthanasia. Press zero for the receptionist.

By the time I was able to press zero, what was I thinking about? Dying dogs. It was literally impossible to call my vet without thinking about the fact that, someday, my dogs will be old and I may have to make tough choices. It also made me curious to know just how many calls she was getting about end-of-life services that it would merit a spot on the menu before appointment requests.

While some might consider it a minor thing, I couldn't help thinking that, if my vet gave the thumbs-up to this message (or, worse, wasn't aware of the message every caller to her clinic was greeted with), she might be making other bad decisions, too. Was she—or might she be at any point in the future—dropping the ball when it came to my dogs' care?

We've all heard the adage that the way you do anything is the way you do everything. That's why there are no minor details in the grand scheme of things. It's far too easy for customers to make an assumption or determination about a lot based on a little.

Everything is experience. Something as seemingly insignificant as a voicemail menu says a lot more to your customers and your prospects than just which number to dial. This is also the prime reason why *everyone* at a company is in the experience department, whether they know it or not.

I decided to find a new vet and asked for recommendations in my neighborhood's Facebook group. I made an appointment at an office that had lots of enthusiastic advocates. I knew I was in the right place when I saw a sign in the exam room that said, "ATTENTION: For your convenience and your pet's comfort, we are now facilitating payment while you and your pet are still in the exam room. SIT. STAY! Thank you."

Crystal Baller

It's amazing the things that matter to us when we have pets. From the time we brought our second rescue pup, Bandit, home from the humane society, he's been a little . . . different. He's a sweet dog, but he's anxious and prone to incessant barking and digging, among other less-than-desirable behaviors.

One afternoon, I was lamenting to a friend over lunch how I wasn't sure what to do next. We'd already hired a trainer, a pet behavioralist, and a guy who called himself "the Doggie Lama" and suggested we use an alpha voice to threaten Bandit into submission. We ignored the latter, but the formers' collective efforts hadn't been very effective either, and we were running out of things to try.

"I've got the answer," my lunch date replied matter-of-factly. "You need to take him to see my dog psychic."

I couldn't tell if she was joking, so I sat in silence. She wasn't joking. She told me how the psychic had been responsible for major changes in her dog's behavior.

"The only thing," she said, "is that you might have to wait a while. He books up months in advance."

I immediately emailed him about a consultation, unsure of what to expect, but also unsure of what else to try. A few days later, he called while I was out with another friend. He told me he'd love to meet Bandit, and he could fit me in about six months later. When I hung up, clearly disappointed, my friend said, "Was that Frank? I've been taking my dogs to him *for*-ever! I'll text him and ask him to get you in right away."

At this point, I was beyond curious—not just about the experience awaiting me, but also about how many of my friends were taking their pets for psychic readings. Was it a thing everyone is doing now that I just missed the memo on, like intermittent fasting?

The next week, I walked with my husband and Bandit into a colorfully furnished room in an East Nashville home, unsure of what to expect. There were candles and incense burners all around, along with a dog bowl that was formed out of some type of crystal.

As Frank greeted us, he placed his hands on Bandit's face and said, "Well, I can already see one problem, right off the bat."

We waited in suspense as the psychic paused dramatically and then said, "Bandit isn't a dog. He's a wild stallion. And he's simply exhausted from everyone treating him like a dog."

"Well, then, thanks for clearing that up," I thought to myself. I'm rarely at a loss for words, but I had no idea how to respond. Was this how guests on *Maury* felt when he opened the envelope?

The hour that followed was filled with other equally unexpected and unpredictable moments. We asked questions to the medium, and he relayed Bandit's "answers" to us. Why did he continue barking at one neighbor, even though he's seen him hundreds of times? "Because your neighbor is a jerk," Frank deadpanned. Why did he dig so many holes? "He likes to dig."

Bandit, whose anxiety was off the charts when we arrived, was calm and quiet when we left. My husband joked that the crystal water might have been spiked. I wasn't sure what to think, except that it was an experience unlike any I'd ever had before.

Sometimes, keeping customers in the dark about what to expect is a good thing. Especially if you've got a months-long waiting list and advocates telling their friends they "must" buy your product or service. However, for most people trying to sell something, expectations should not be a mystery. Customers are talking to friends, plugging queries into search engines and socials, and reading online reviews. They want to know what to expect from you. Prospects want to know what their item will look like, how many days they should expect to wait for an order to arrive, or what the experience will be like from start to finish.

Regardless of the size of your business, you can follow a three-step process to make exceeding expectations the norm. The process is as follows: map, measure, maximize. Now, let's dig in to each of these. Don't worry, I won't ask you to wipe your paws at the door, and no knowledge of chakras is needed.

1. Map

Are you familiar with customer journey mapping, in which executives and employees (usually with the help of an expensive consultant) work to identify every part of a customer's interaction with a brand? It's a bit like pumpkin spice—it started out as a good thing, but earned a bad reputation when people began taking it waaaaaay too far.

I am a proponent of customer journey mapping. I am *not* a proponent of it being a chore that takes months, costs tens or even hundreds of thousands of dollars, and results in spreadsheets with thousands of cells of information. Data is only useful when it's being *used*. Trying to map every single scenario a customer might encounter with your company is a fool's errand. Even if you do complete the task (which is unlikely, given how fast environmental factors change), there's a very high probability that it will be so overwhelming that neither you nor your employees will use it as an active, living document.

Instead, working to understand common needs and motivations at critical points of interaction is an exercise that can be completed in less than a day—and taught and regularly reviewed in even less time than that. Then, it becomes scalable and accessible to every new team member.

You can create a simple, powerful journey map—what I call the SUPER Map—by plotting the principles you've learned in this book into a grid. Simply consider every step on the Ladder to Superfandom from Chapter 2 and how S, U, P, E, and R intersect with each one.

	[SUB-STAGES]	AWARENESS	ATTRACTION
S START WITH YOUR STORY	Sharing Your Story		
	Showcasing Your Uniqueness		
U UNDERSTAND YOUR CUSTOMER'S STORY	Needs		
	Motivations		
	Emotions		
P PERSONALIZE	Touchpoints		
	Interactions		
	Team Members		
E EXCEED EXPECTATIONS	Most Important Moments		
	Opportunities to Optimize		
R REPEAT	Measure		
	Maximize		
	Automate		
APATHY RISKS			

ACTION	ADOPTION	AFFINITY	ADVOCACY

You can customize this template as needed, adding further sub-stages or important customer considerations. Just don't get too carried away. Remember, the goal is to create a map your employees will both *understand* and *refer to*. If you run a three-person accounting practice and you put together a map that looks like it was pulled from the operations manual of a Boeing Dreamliner, you've overcomplicated the exercise. SUPER is simple, and simple is SUPER.

After helping thousands of people create journey maps over the past decade, I've observed that many professionals have a pretty good intuitive feel for the "during" part of a transactional relationship but don't pay enough attention to the "before" and "after."

Let's say you operate a life insurance agency in your hometown. "During" represents the time when you're talking to a prospect about insurance—you're getting to know them, gathering quotes, awaiting their decision, and so on. "Before" is all the parts of the customer journey that you *weren't* there for—the online searches they did, or the visit to your website and the website of a competitor. "After" is everything that happens once the transaction is finished: Are you staying in touch with your customers? Reaching out with helpful information at the right time? Regardless of your industry, your customers shouldn't only hear from you when you're back to ask for more money (for example, when it's time for renewals, or there's a premium increase, or you're responding to a submitted claim).

Consider your own buying behaviors and it's easy to see why "before" is so important. If you're anything like me, once you get a recommendation from someone (either a personal contact or from a review online), you do more research. Whether you're looking for additional social proof or just the information you need to pull the trigger, you're making decisions before you ever interact with a person or a chatbot. "Before" is your chance to set yourself apart from every competitor out there by sharing your story.

The "after" is critical because it's so much easier and cheaper to sell something to someone *again* than it is to sell something to a new customer for the first time. It's also where all the relational gold happens. One repeatable, memorable action that triggers an experience for your customer at the end of every transaction can mean the difference between a one-time customer and a lifelong superfan.

2. Measure

Albert Einstein once said, "Not everything that can be counted counts, and not everything that counts can be counted." Smart guy, that Einstein. He was correct.

You can't know for sure if you're exceeding customers' expectations unless you measure their feedback in some way. Metrics like NPS (net promoter score), CSAT (customer satisfaction), CES (customer effort score), and EGR (earned growth rate) are all helpful in specific situations, especially to track changes in customer sentiment over time.

My two favorite metrics for measuring customer experience are CSAT, which happens in the moment or immediately after an interaction, and EGR, which is a measure of the revenue coming from repeat and referred customers over time. Because effective CX measurement varies so much from company to company, I've compiled an in-depth overview at BrittanyHodak.com/SUPER. Check it out, and let me know if it *measures* up. (Can't stop, won't stop!)

You can also go low-tech to measure customer experience. I went to a new dentist recently, and one of the pieces of paper on the check-in clipboard of forms said, "How did you hear about us?" I checked the "referred by a friend" box and wrote the name of the friend who'd suggested the practice. During my visit, the hygienist, receptionist, *and* dentist welcomed me to the practice and said nice things about my friend Sadie who'd sent me there.

They didn't just create a form for the sake of a form. They read it. In the moment. And responded appropriately. It doesn't take a lot of money, or even a lot of effort, to design and implement systems to gain valuable information about your customers.

Dayspring Pens' TJ Stinnett once told me that his company doesn't keep track of mistakes in terms of percentages ("98.6 percent correct") but instead in a dashboard that shows true numbers ("14 incorrect orders this week"). Why? Because every order represents a customer, and it's more impactful to see those customers represented as numbers than as percentages. In his words, "Many of our purchases are gifts, and every order represents a gift we were entrusted to get exactly right to mark an important occasion in someone's life."

TJ and the team look at the numbers on a dashboard daily. "Each of us is always striving for 100 percent perfection. Even if it's something minor, like the wrong font being used, we count it as an error and work hard to make it right."

TJ's story illustrates why measuring and displaying data in more than one way can be profoundly impactful. It's a great daily reminder that those dashboard statistics aren't just numbers—they're people.

Here is a low-tech method you can use to begin "measuring" today, no calculators or computer programs needed. I devised it because, as someone who cried *every night* during my semester of advanced statistics in grad school, uncomplicated formulas are all I can condone in good conscience.

For every one-to-one interaction you have, there are three possible outcomes for the other person. At the end of the exchange, they'll feel better, worse, or the same as they did before. I refer to these outcomes as net positive (better), net negative (worse), and net neutral (same).

Here's a secret to not only great customer experience, but also to making your entire life better: try to make as many interactions as possible net positive experiences. If you can do that, so many of the other things will fall into place.

If people leave most interactions with you feeling better than they did before, you will naturally build a reputation as someone people want to do business with. Your customers, your colleagues, your vendors, and even your acquaintances will want to work with you more because *they feel better* by doing so.

Think about your own interactions with people. Isn't it true that you find yourself naturally gravitating toward interactions where you feel better at the end? We've *all* got those friends who can be emotionally draining and only call when they want or need something.

Business is no different. People will remember the companies, colleagues, and associates who make things easy. They'll say things like, "Wow, that was so much easier than I expected!" or, "You took care of it so quickly." Making interactions feel as effortless as possible not only exceeds expectations but also increases the likelihood that customers will come back or tell their friends . . . maybe even that one friend who only calls when they need something.

Can you turn every interaction into a net positive? No. You will inevitably find yourself in situations where you must deliver bad news. But, by focusing on creating a net neutral outcome for your customer instead of a net negative one, you can improve the situation for everyone. Think of possible solutions before you deliver bad news. Be prepared to share your thoughtful plans B, C, and D, then showcase your active listening skills to turn an otherwise-net-negative situation around. Work hard to leave a path of net positive experiences in your wake, and people will notice.

You may never realize the impact that some of your net positive interactions have on your customers and colleagues. Three days after I quit my well-paying job in advertising to launch my first startup, I

EXPERIENCE

IS

EVERYTHING

★ ★ ★ ★ ★ AND ★ ★ ★ ★ ★

EVERYTHING

IS

EXPERIENCE

had a phone interview scheduled with Keith Urban for a project I was working on for the Academy of Country Music Awards.

After we finished our conversation, I thanked Keith for his time and gave him the CliffsNotes version of what the interview had been for. He seemed genuinely interested and graciously asked several follow-up questions about my new venture. I admitted he was the first artist I'd talked to, this was the first major project, and I was more than a bit nervous about life as an entrepreneur.

He gave me some words of encouragement, including telling me what a great idea he thought the company was, and wished me well on the journey. His encouragement helped me through the tough weeks and months that followed as I questioned the viability of my young business.

About five years later, I was interviewing Keith again—this time in person for a *Forbes* story—and I told him how much his words had meant years earlier. He shared a story with me about receiving a similar confidence boost in the early days of his own career, when it seemed no label in Nashville would take a chance on him. He said he replayed those kind words in his head in many dark hours.

You may never witness the impact a few kind words can have on others, whether you're in their life for years or just a few minutes. Net positive experiences often don't cost anything to deliver, but their value can be priceless.

3. Maximize

I understand that "every interaction matters" sounds overwhelming. That's where the third step comes in. Look for opportunities to create moments of "wow" to elevate the ordinary to the extraordinary. Be so good in those strategic, repeatable moments that your customers can't wait to come back. One memorable "wow" moment can help erase the sting of minor annoyances along the way, so be intentional in your experience design.

Let's take hotels, for example. Some are highly commoditized and others are highly differentiated. I've been lucky enough to travel extensively as a keynote speaker, staying in some of the most beautiful and luxurious properties in the world. After a while, a lot of them blur together. I don't recall which sheets were the softest, which pillows were the fluffiest, or whose room service chocolate cake was the best.

What I *do* recall are the experiences. I'll never forget how excited Kadoh was when Snoopy came into our hotel room to do a bedtime tuck-in at Knott's Berry Farm Hotel in California. Every time we're in Southern California, we go back because of that single experience. Lots of hotels have amazing spas or Michelin-starred restaurants. Give me a costumed character who will come hug my kids and tuck them in at bedtime.

Another amazing example is the Popsicle Hotline at the Magic Castle Hotel in L.A. It's a fancy phone line staffed around the clock where pool guests can order a free popsicle, delivered by an employee in white gloves on a silver platter. It's a "wow" moment that maximizes the impact of a customer's experience with your entire brand.

My favorite hotel chain to check into, by far, is the Margaritaville resorts. Even before you have your room key, an aloha-shirt-clad team member will make sure you've got a complimentary rum punch in your hands, if rum punch is your thing.

You can even use moment maximization to turn around something that might otherwise be a negative. On a recent visit to the LEGOLAND Resort in Florida, I was as mesmerized as my kids were each time we stepped into the elevator. It was adorned with floor-to-ceiling decals of dancing, human-sized LEGO characters and a disco ball hanging from the ceiling. When the doors closed, flashing lights blanketed the elevator and music from ABBA and the Bee Gees piped through a speaker. It was so fun that we didn't notice how *slow* the ride was until about our fifth time in the elevator. Even then, we didn't mind because every ride was a blast.

LEGOLAND took a potential annoyance (a slow elevator) and turned it into an experience we'll remember for years. That's the magic of intentional experience design. What's the slow elevator in your business, and how can you transform it into a disco party?

Each of these examples has marginal costs associated with it, but the ROI in repeat customers and referrals makes the investment more than worth it. The cost of a costumed character or a staffer passing out popsicles is a very inexpensive way to get repeat bookings. I'm not sure how much LEGOLAND is paying for the rights to play "Dancing Queen" and "Stayin' Alive" in the elevators, but I'm sure it's nothing compared to the $600/night we paid for our adventure-themed rooms.

When you create standout experiences, your customers will remember. They'll come back. They'll tell their friends. Much like gremlins, superfan customers multiply into more customers . . . and you don't even have to get them wet.

◄◄ SUPERQUICK! REWIND ◄◄

Everything is experience and experience is everything. Follow a three-step process to make exceeding expectations the norm:

1   Map the most impactful interactions that you can elevate into memorable experiences at key parts of your customer's journey.

2   Measure the moments to track how your customers are feeling.

3   Maximize important moments to create the can't-stop-talking-about-it experiences your customers come back for… and share.

12

Hanging by a Moment

· · · · · · · · · · · · · · · · · ·

If you want your business to be successful,
customer experience needs to shift from being a
line item on a "to do" list to being a way of life.
JOEY COLEMAN

D O YOU HAVE an older sibling? If so, when you were growing up, did you often feel like *everything* you did was being compared to what they did?

I've got bad news for you: it ain't over. And it's worse now. In an experience economy, people aren't just comparing you to your direct competitors. They're comparing you to the best experiences they've had with anyone, *period*. If your customer is experiencing delays in logistics or shipping, they aren't going to think, "Well, I'm sure they are trying their best." They're going to think, "If Domino's can show me where my pizza is in real time, why can't this company get [your thing] right?"

In that moment, they will decide whether to continue to do business with you or to find another solution. Annoyance quickly snowballs into anger, apathy, or abandonment . . . and sometimes all of the above.

How Good It Can Get

Whether you're selling Mazdas or monkey wrenches, it's about more than just the product or the service. Your "thing" is far from the only thing that matters. Let's say you're a massage therapist. The massage techniques you learned in school are only one small part of the overall equation. Even if the only time *you* encounter the customer is when they're on your table, it's only one part of the journey for them.

How simple was it to book an appointment? Could they do it online, or did they have to call someone? If they had to make a phone call, how were they greeted? Were the various options for services clearly listed somewhere, along with their prices? When the appointment was booked, did they get a confirmation email and an option to automatically add the appointment details to their calendar?

How about the day of the service? Was it easy to find the location? Is your business information up to date with Google and Apple for people who search in Maps? Were parking and check-in directions obvious? How about the temperature and comfort of the lobby?

Will your client find a standard massage table in the room, or a heated one? Is there a luxurious robe waiting on the back of the door? Do they have the option to choose what music is playing, and how loudly? What about any essential oils being diffused in the room or integrated into the treatment?

I could keep going, but you get the idea. Eliminating minor annoyances and maximizing comfort is an important part of differentiating yourself from your competitors. Even incremental improvements in customer experience can lead to exponential increases in customer retention.

The same is true for package design. Every square inch is an opportunity to settle for standard or differentiate yourself with excellence.

Are you frustrating your customers with that nearly impossible to open hard plastic shelling around your product? Or what about those annoying plastic tabs in clothes that you must cut apart? Stickers that never come off, or that leave goopy residue?

Intentional experience design means examining *every* part of a customer's experience and looking for ways to improve upon it, from the time your category first pops into their mind until they've been a loyal customer for decades. It builds on everything you learned in the last chapter. Once you've got the hang of mapping, measuring, and maximizing, you'll be creating magic everywhere.

Hard to Forget

It's not just the grand gestures that people remember. Have you ever eaten at a Moe's Southwest Grill? As soon as you walk through the doors, employees shout, "Welcome to Moe's!" You're greeted with energy and enthusiasm even before you have a chance to see wall décor bearing messages like "Hear me out: Queso lazy river."

Armoire is a subscription clothing rental company for female executives that offers in-house stylists who help curate looks for members. When an order of clothing ships to subscribers, the package arrives tied in a piece of twine and completed with an origami dress printed on beautiful paper.

Being a parent has taught me a lot about intentional experience design (and a million other things), including that there's no detail too small to build an experience on, and no experience you can't improve with a little creativity. My youngest son, Jones, is two years old. Any normal activity can transform into a fun experience simply by singing his favorite song, "If You're Happy and You Know It." I can tell the kid to put on his shirt six times in a row and he wouldn't move a muscle. But if I *sing* "If you're happy and you know it, put on your shirt!" he can't get his arms through those holes fast enough, and he's smiling and giggling the entire time.

For every touchpoint, ask yourself, "Is there something I can do to elevate this interaction to a memorable experience?" It doesn't have to be complicated, or even cost a lot of money. My kids are thrilled when they're offered a sticker or a lollipop when they accompany me through a checkout lane. I'm always delighted when I'm offered an upgrade at a hotel or rental car counter. My husband's favorite part of our date nights at Olive Garden is the little chocolate mint that comes with the check.

You don't have to focus on one-size-fits-all solutions, either. Especially if you're serving a diverse customer base. McDonald's draws in millions of pop culture lovers with its rotating slate of celebrity-inspired meals. Meanwhile, kids who've never heard of the celebrities who rep for McDonald's beg to stop when they see the Golden Arches because of the licensed Happy Meal toys or the PlayPlace playground. And, of course, the special offers in the McDonald's app and its bargain menus appeal to budget-conscious customers. None of these campaigns interferes with the others because they're all designed to connect with (and exceed the expectations of) different customers. You can connect more than one of your stories with more than one community of customers simultaneously.

Easy on Me

Regularly audit every part of your customers' journeys to look for ways to simplify their experiences. Are there six options on your phone tree when there only needs to be three? Do you greet every

WHAT CAN I DO TO

ELEVATE

THIS INTERACTION

★ ★ ★ ★ ★ INTO A ★ ★ ★ ★ ★

MEMORABLE

EXPERIENCE?

customer at your medical practice with eight paper forms to fill out, making them rewrite their name, address, and insurance information on each page? Are you requiring extra clicks on mobile because your site is optimized for desktop screens? If you want to make money, make things easy.

Convenience has never been more important. I remember my parents paying for groceries with paper checks. They would fill out the check right there at the register, and we'd wait as the cashier cross-referenced the address on their driver's licenses against the check. That wasn't even thirty years ago. Today, I get annoyed if I have to remove my credit card from my wallet because the RFID machine doesn't work when I wave my phone near it.

My friends and I used to wait for hours to download songs on dial-up internet. Now, not only do my kids just *ask the air* to play literally any song that's ever existed, they even get annoyed when Alexa or Siri doesn't get it right on the first attempt. My four-year-old still remarks when a business has an "old-timey door" that doesn't open automatically. "Looks like we'll have to use the doorknob like people did in the olden days," he'll say.

Expectations are always increasing and, as kids who grew up with technology (and automatic doors) get older, they'll demand even more innovation and convenience from the businesses they support.

I was traveling through the Dallas Fort Worth Airport not long ago and noticed screens outside each terminal restroom updating in real time to advise passersby on the number of empty stalls inside and the distance to the nearest restrooms in both directions. Inside, red and green lights above each stall door broadcast the availability so travelers aren't trying to peek under the doors.

Innovate before you have to. Don't wait for your competitors to upgrade the category in which you operate. There are always ways to improve your customers' experiences. Just because "good enough" was good enough in the past, that is no guarantee it will be tomorrow. If you're not actively looking for ways to improve things for your customers, you can bet a competitor will come along pretty soon and do it for you.

◀◀ SUPERQUICK! REWIND ◀◀

Every component of your experience is an extension of your story and can impact the likelihood of a buyer coming back or making a referral. Identify the interactions that you can make more convenient or comfortable for your customers, and don't settle for a one-size-fits-all solution.

13

Back 2 Good

. . . .

Mistakes are a fact of life. It is
the response to the error that counts.

NIKKI GIOVANNI

EW THINGS in life are more useless—or more deceptively named—than the "Recall This Message" button in Microsoft Outlook.

Unlike a real "Undo Send" button (thanks again for that, Gmail!), "Recall This Message" doesn't pull back your email from the depths of cyberspace or make it self-destruct in the unintended recipient's inbox unless something like fifty-three parameters match up perfectly. For example, it must still be unopened by all recipients . . . and they must all be using the same email server.

Even then, the stupid feature just sends *another* email saying something like (and I'm paraphrasing here), "Oh, hello there! The sender would like to recall the email they just sent you by mistake because something in it makes them look like a jerk. So, you know, maybe be nice and don't look at it." Which, of course, makes 99.9 percent of the human population open the "recalled" email immediately to see what's inside.

Why this diatribe? Because I'm still haunted by what might be the most facepalm moment of my entire career. I was working at a record company and part of my responsibilities included setting up promotions with retail partners. Late one Friday, I was trying to finish up when an artist manager emailed me and a few others saying she'd secured an expensive autographed guitar for a giveaway with a big mall retailer.

I quickly wrote back saying that that particular mall retailer had a terrible open rate on their emails and offered basically nothing in stores in exchange for contest items. Plus, their marketing team was difficult to work with. Instead, I said, we'd be much better served by offering it as a prize at a competitive store whose reach was much higher and whose team was more accommodating. I suggested we talk about it Monday when I could make the full case for why the marketing campaign would be significantly more successful at the second retailer.

It wasn't until I hit "send" that I saw the artist manager had copied the head of marketing and the buyer for the original retailer on the email. I was mortified! My embarrassment and frustration only grew as I found myself helplessly navigating "Recall Email" purgatory, praying for a miracle.

I saw my entire career flash before my twenty-three-year-old eyes. This was it. I would be fired. The artist manager would hate me, obviously. And so much for my relationship with the retailer... that was clearly over.

I spent the next few minutes reeling in my empty office, writing a dizzying flurry of apology emails in a desperate attempt to save my job. A few minutes later, my desk phone rang. The artist manager's name scrolled across the caller ID. I was positive she was calling to scream at me, but I held my breath and picked up. Instead of screaming, she was laughing. "We've all been there," she said. "Don't worry about it.

By the way, it's 9 p.m. on a Friday and you're still at the office. Leave! We'll square everything away on Monday."

It was a very long weekend. I kept expecting to get fired via email. "I guess they're waiting to do it in person," I thought to myself on the downtown 6 Train on Monday morning.

As it turns out, the email was barely on my boss's radar. He responded similarly to how the artist manager had. "It sucks, but it happens to all of us at some point," he told me. "Now, go make it right with the retailer."

Luckily, the buyer and marketing manager at the mall were gracious and forgiving. They even acknowledged that everything I'd said was true and told me they wanted to work with me to improve communication and the impact of their promotions. One of them even joked, "Maybe one day you'll accidentally copy us on an email saying how great we are."

I felt lucky to survive with my job and relationships intact. As I got older, I realized that the situation wasn't that atypical. I learned a few valuable lessons from the flub. First: Never, *ever* use "reply all" unless you've triple-checked the recipient list. Second: Customers don't expect you to be perfect all the time. They expect you to try your best and to fix things when they go wrong.

No one is perfect. And here's the thing—being *imperfect* can work to your advantage because it can connect you to your customers in a way that months or even years of perfect service can't. The term "service recovery paradox" was first used in 1992 to describe a common phenomenon when a customer is happier after a mistake has been corrected than they were before the mistake occurred. In other words, experiencing the mistake and the aftermath to fix it made them think more highly of the company. They appreciate you owning up to the error and then making it right.

For What It's Worth
. . . .

How much would you pay to make something right for your best client? How about a first-time client? What's it worth to keep a customer from giving a competitor a try? It's imperative to know the answer to these questions ahead of time, so you aren't scrambling in the moment.

When things go wrong it's better to make a customer happy than to make a profit. Of course, there are many factors that go into individual decisions, but try to approach every instance thinking about the lifetime value of the customer and not just the value of the single transaction. Empower people within the organization to make decisions to fix problems before they escalate, even if it means offering a full refund.

I'll never forget when my dad banned us from shopping at Sears. He was mowing the yard one Sunday afternoon and his push mower broke. He decided it was finally time to get a riding lawn mower and, after consulting the ads in the Sunday paper, he and I jumped into the truck and headed to Sears to pick one up.

When we arrived, the associates at Sears told my dad they were out of the model in the ad and wouldn't get any more in until the middle of the week. "What about this one right here?" he asked, pointing to a display model on the sales floor.

"We can't sell you that one," a salesperson answered. "It's the display model."

"Don't you offer assembly?" my dad asked. They confirmed that they did, in fact, offer assembly for $50. "So," my dad asked, "why can't you sell me this one, charge me $50 for assembly, and build a new floor model when you get your shipment in?"

The salesperson said that wasn't possible. My dad politely asked to speak to someone who might be able to approve an exception. When the manager arrived, my dad explained that his only day off was Sunday and, if he couldn't mow the yard today, it would be a week before he got another chance.

The manager told my dad that it was against policy to sell store models before the end of the season, even at full price plus the cost of assembly, and even though assembly happened on-site.

When we walked out of the store without a new mower, my dad told me we'd never spend another penny at Sears. He vowed that he wouldn't even be returning his Craftsman tools for free replacements when they broke.

Dad's workshop was filled with Craftsman tools. Our closets were packed with clothes bearing the Sears private-label brands and our kitchen was filled with Kenmore appliances. But from that day forward, shopping at Sears was prohibited. My mom canceled her Sears credit card account. We took our name off the mailing list for the famous catalog. Even if we had to drive farther or spend more, we went somewhere else. "Sears doesn't want our money, and we aren't going to give it to them," Dad said more than once.

While I can't say definitively whether my dad's stance played a direct role in the company going bankrupt three decades later, I *can* say that it made a lasting impression on me. Why should a customer continue to do business with a company that doesn't seem to want to do business with them?

Customers *deserve* to work with customer-centric companies and, now more than ever, they're demanding it. Smart businesses of all sizes know that if they don't take good care of their customers, someone else will come along and do it for them.

IF YOU DON'T

TAKE CARE OF

YOUR CUSTOMERS

★ SOMEONE ELSE ★

WILL DO IT

★ ★ ★ FOR YOU ★ ★ ★

Sorry Doesn't Always Make It Right

Customer centricity isn't only important when things are going right. It's about repairing the relationship when things go wrong, too, and ensuring that a customer feels valued and heard. When that involves an apology, there's a right and a wrong way to do it. Actually, there are *lots* of bad ways to apologize ... and many of them end up with you being in a worse position than you were before you started.

There are five steps to a proper apology—the 5 As. Together, they constitute the correct way to make amends.

1. Acknowledge

Many of us have been on the receiving end of a "Whatever I did to make you mad, I'm sorry." We know exactly what it feels like: A BS un-apology. For an apology to feel authentic, you must begin by acknowledging what went wrong.

"I realize that we're three days past the delivery window I promised. I can imagine how frustrating this must be," or "I understand that our error has caused significant disruption to your event, which I know is unacceptable." Own up to the failure at hand and how it negatively impacted your prospect or customer, and how they are likely feeling as a result.

2. Apologize

The second A of apologizing is perhaps the most obvious: the actual apology. Say "I'm sorry," and mean it. One of my favorite Benjamin Franklin quotes is "Never ruin an apology with an excuse." It was good advice when he said it, and it's held up over time. Customers don't want excuses—at least not as part of the apology. "I'm sorry" is a complete sentence. No qualifiers, and no excuses.

It's also worth noting that a company can't be sorry because a company is not a person (regardless of what the Supreme Court says). Companies do not have emotions or feelings. So, if you find yourself writing an apology email or note, *never* sign it with just the company name. You can sign it with your name, followed by "on behalf of everyone at . . ." or something to that effect, but don't ever use just a company name. That makes it impersonal (by definition) and less meaningful to your customer.

Another no-no is comparing any customer's experience to that of another. Just don't—ever! You might think it sounds better to say something like, "This never happens. We process more than 10,000 transactions per day, and 9,999 of them are perfect," but your customer doesn't care about anyone else's experience. If anything, comparisons make situations worse, not better.

Imagine you were in a relationship and your significant other said, "I can't believe you think I'm cheating on you! I've dated lots of people, and none of them ever complained." How would that go over? Exactly. Don't compare any customer's experience to that of any other customer.

3. Ask

We covered active listening in Chapter 8. You're going to put those skills to work again as part of your apology. Ask, "How can I make this right?" and then give your customer the opportunity to tell you. They might propose something along the lines of what you have in mind, or an entirely different idea. Regardless, it's important to give the person you've wronged in some way the opportunity to suggest what you can do to make it right. By inviting them into the process, you increase the likelihood that they will be satisfied with the outcome.

4. Atone

This is where you put the solution into action. Show your customer that you don't just walk the walk but that you talk the talk, too. If you're working as part of a customer service department where the solutions are somewhat standardized, you can combine the third step, *ask*, with the fourth, *atone*.

Even if you've got a predetermined idea of what should be done to fix the issue, giving your customer the opportunity to respond to your offer is critical. That might sound something like, "I'm going to get a replacement part overnighted to you today, at no cost. I'm also crediting your account $25 for the inconvenience. How does that sound to you?"

5. Adjust

Once you've resolved your customer's problem, the final part of each apology should be to adjust whatever system, process, or behavior (or lack thereof) led to the problem in the first place. Sometimes the adjustment will be obvious (a human or system failure), and others will take longer to diagnose and correct. Either way, don't move so quickly from fire to fire that you fail to notice there's someone on your team throwing lit matches.

It may be appropriate to share what you'll be adjusting with your customers. If you know the issue and can quickly troubleshoot what you'll be amending, include it as part of the atonement phase. "I see now that this was caused by an error in our payment processing system. I've notified my CTO and CFO, who have promised to have the issue resolved within twenty-four hours." Other times, the adjustment may happen entirely behind closed doors. Either way, make sure you don't speed past this step, or you might find yourself in a *Groundhog Day* situation, solving the same problem over and over and over again.

There are few issues you can't overcome with a sincere, proper apology. That annoyed or upset customer might just become a loyal advocate after they experience firsthand how much you care and how hard you're working to solve their problem. And if not?

Don't Go Away Mad (Just Go Away)

Some customers are hostile, belligerent, or otherwise awful, and no company or business owner should be afraid to stand up to those customers with a clear and simple message: We don't want or need your business. Goodbye.

The adage that "the customer is always right" is not only incorrect and outdated, it's also potentially harmful in its widespread acceptance. The customer *isn't* always right. And, sometimes, a customer simply isn't right for your business. Should you be empathic and understanding with customers? Yes. But being accommodating and apologetic when merited is not the same thing as being abused. Here are a few ways to successfully walk that line.

Don't let bad customers cost you good employees

While customers are entitled to complain or to voice legitimate concerns, if those complaints turn combative, it's a problem. Everyone has bad days—and some businesses are accustomed to dealing with customers who are at the worst moments of their lives (divorce attorneys, funeral homes, and the like)—but there's a difference between a customer having a bad day and a customer being abusive (or a straight-up bad person).

If you don't stand up for your employees (and yourself) when customers are repeatedly antagonistic, it will breed problems on multiple fronts. For starters, employees can only support customers if they are first supported by the rest of their team. If you allow *bad* customers to be abusive, your employees can feel unappreciated and will be more likely to provide inferior service to *all* customers, good and bad alike. Additionally, while some employees will put up with abuse, others will quit to find an environment where they're more supported.

In addition to demoralizing employees, bad customers also steal resources away from good customers. Dealing with bad apples means expending efforts that could be otherwise directed to serving *good* customers. If you've been on a flight with a drunk passenger, you've seen this firsthand. The flight attendants are forced to spend a disproportionate amount of time, energy, and attention on the jerk who's out of line.

Don't keep fighting losing battles

Some customers will never, *ever* be happy. The quicker you cut your losses and run, the sooner you can move on. They drive you crazy... and drive down your profit margins and employee satisfaction.

I was at a big Super Bowl party in Manhattan in 2011 when the Giants beat the Patriots and, for about ten minutes, all the New York fans were thrilled. But by the time the post-game show was over, two fans at the party were totally disgruntled. "Great—we're going to get the last draft pick now," one said. "Yeah, which really stinks, because I bet so-and-so and someone-else are going to retire now that they've got their rings," said the other. Their team *won the Super Bowl*, and yet these self-proclaimed "fans" were bitter and feeling sorry for themselves half an hour later. Go figure.

Don't be afraid to "fire" bad customers

Bad customers will always cost you more than they're worth. How do you fire them? First, do it calmly. Even if a customer is nasty, explain that, due to the gap between their expectations and yours, the relationship just isn't going to work out.

Second, be as clear as possible. Is your relationship over effective immediately? Upon delivery of outstanding assets? At the end of the month, quarter, or year? Be clear and definitive, both in your description of how your relationship will end and what will happen next.

Third, make the transition as simple as possible. If you expect to end relationships with more than a couple of customers over the course of the year, it might be helpful to put together a list of companies or professionals who provide similar services to the ones you've been performing for your customer. This not only allows you to say something like, "These providers might be a better fit for the goals you have over the next year," or however you want to word it, but it also lets you end the relationship on a helpful note.

Last, be decisive. Once you've decided a customer or client relationship is over, it needs to be over. No trial separations, no "let's give it some time and see how we feel" nonsense, and no back-pedaling. Rip off the Band-Aid. There are too many *great* customers, both current and future, to waste any more of your time and energy on the wrong ones. Plus, bad customers rarely, if ever, make good referrals . . . they just invite more unhappy customers.

◀◀ SUPERQUICK! REWIND ◀◀

You will inevitably make mistakes when working with customers, so it's important to have contingency plans in place. If you train your team on how to apologize with the 5 As—acknowledge, apologize, ask, atone, and adjust—they will be better equipped to handle any apology appropriately.

Despite conventional wisdom, the customer is *not* always right. Bad customers suck the time, energy, and enthusiasm away from your employees and can ruin the experience for the good customers. Kindly show them the door before they drain additional resources.

Repetition makes reputa-
tion and reputation makes
customers.

ELIZABETH ARDEN

PART 6

REPEAT

14

Here I Go Again

. . . .

Be customer-obsessed. Your customer
relationships are only as good as the quality
of your communication and engagement.
JOE WELU

EVERY TIME I hear a businessperson say something like, "What I do for a customer could never be automated!" I wonder if telephone switchboard operators from the 1930s and '40s ever thought that. You know, the ones who picked up the phone and moved the cables from one knob to another to connect calls. Did they think they had job security?

How about telegraph operators? Film projectionists? Door-to-door encyclopedia salespeople?

Technology will continue to eliminate jobs, just as it has done for centuries. From farms to factories to freight companies, there's no denying that technology is constantly transforming roles.

I believe the impact of technology in knowledge-based industries will be different. In many cases, people won't be replaced by technology outright—at least not in the next several decades. Instead, people who *don't* embrace technology to help them accomplish the goals of their customers will be replaced by people who *do*.

There is no reason to allocate time to tasks that, if automated, do not negatively impact a customer's experience. The introduction of technology to roles frees up more time to focus on the *human* side of the business: the things that can't be automated—at least not yet.

One of the best ways to free up more of your time for high-value tasks is by removing lower-value tasks from your day. Automation is not the enemy. We're fortunate to be living in this moment in history when many tasks can be done for us, by machines, without us even having to ask.

Sometimes we like to think we're adding value to a task when we're not. When I purchased my first robot vacuum cleaner, I was so excited that I named it (which is a normal thing everyone does, right?). As part of the setup process, the app prompted me to set a cleaning schedule. I thought, "Schedule cleanings for the same time every day? Pass. I'll decide when to clean the floors."

Wanna know a secret? I never remembered to clean the floors. Once or twice a week, when I could visibly see dog hair on the hardwood, I turned on the vacuum. Once I was honest with myself about adding no real value to the process, I scheduled regular vacuum runs in the app, and my floors looked awesome! All I had to do was empty the catch container once or twice a month when the app sent me a reminder to do so.

Bye, Bye, Bye

Don't be afraid to admit that a process can work better without your direct involvement in it, and don't be afraid to leverage technology to help you save time. Automation is not the only way to free up more time to focus on higher-value activities. In his viral TED Talk "How to Multiply Your Time," my friend Rory Vaden suggests asking yourself these questions about every task on your to-do list:

- Can you eliminate it?
- If not, can you automate it?
- If not, can you delegate it or teach someone else to do it?

Eliminate tasks that don't add value and reallocate that time to other tasks. Delegate things you hate or that can be performed at a much lower hourly rate than your time merits. Use your newfound precious minutes and hours each week to focus on repeatable activities that turn customers into superfans.

You might be amazed by what it's possible to automate these days. And no, I'm not just talking about room-service robots or autonomous delivery drones. I'm a huge fan of handwritten cards, and while my favorite will always be the cards I write and send myself, I've got apps on my phone that automate the process for me. Customers still get a real card in the mail, with a real stamp and real handwriting, but the handwriting is performed by a robot, not by me.

I wish I had time to send handwritten cards to everyone I want to, but a technology-aided handwritten card is better than no card at all. And saving five minutes per card adds up over the course of a month.

Do I still send actual handwritten cards sometimes? Of course. But, not to everyone, and not in every situation. I'm leveraging technology to help where it's needed and staying involved in places I know I can add value. This allows me to reach even more customers than if I wasn't using technology while continuing to focus time and energy on high-value (and high-potential) relationships.

Automation doesn't have to be all or nothing. Figure out what works best for you. Just don't be afraid to admit it when you're no longer adding value to a system or process. Recognize that as a good thing and assign yourself a higher-value job doing something else to serve your customers.

Check Yes or No

Not every task will be something you can automate, but I have another hack for you. What if I told you that you could begin using one of the most powerful pieces of productivity software ever created, right now, for free? What if the software had next to no learning curve, could be immediately customized to fit your exact needs, and was simple to optimize and update daily? Oh, and using it would increase your odds of success dramatically.

Are you interested? Awesome! Because the product in question isn't an app—it's a checklist. That's right: a simple checklist can help set you apart from the competition and help you crush your goals.

Comedian Jon Stewart once quipped, "I watch a lot of astronaut movies. Mostly *Star Wars*. And even Han and Chewie use a checklist." Checklists are an invaluable tool for creating superfans.

Whether you prefer to keep up with reminders in a paper notebook, a digital notebook, a list app, your calendar, your CRM, or a project management tool, the best system for a checklist is the one you will *use*. The important thing is to pick a system, customize it so it works for you, and trust the process. Review and revise on a regular basis so that you're constantly improving. Don't trust yourself to remember everything! Get the ideas, tasks, and reminders out of your head and into your list.

The first checklist you create should be a checklist of all the checklists you need to create. A little meta, I know.

As I noted in Chapter 11, many people allocate a disproportionate amount of effort to the "during" phase. Convert a prospect into a

— EVEN —

SANTA CLAUS

CHECKS

— HIS LISTS —

★ TWICE ★

customer. Convert another prospect into another customer. Rinse and repeat. Solve a customer's ticket, move on. Solve another customer's ticket, move on. However, rethinking your workflow to give more attention to the "before" and "after" phases of each interaction can have a compounding effect that's beneficial for you *and* your customers.

Let's say you operate a local art-house movie theater. The "during" phase is when a patron is at your venue. Is the temperature right? How's the popcorn? Are the seats clean? Yes, that's important. But they might not ever *get* there if the "before" isn't right. Are the directions on your website easy to find and understand? Is there information about how to get tickets and where to park? "After" is key too, since you want to get people *back* to the theater again. Are you sending a "thank you" email with an offer for a free concession item on their next visit? Do you have a loyalty program to reward your frequent guests? What about a forum for customers to suggest future films?

Every time I create a new checklist, I evaluate its effectiveness right after using it. Do any items need to be added? Removed? Is more explanation needed to turn this list into part of a playbook for someone else on my team to use, either now or in the future?

It's very rare to get a list exactly right when you first create it. Even Santa Claus checks his lists twice! So don't worry if you don't think of everything right away. It's much easier to build systems as you're solving problems than to do a big brain dump of everything that could hypothetically be important at the onset. Start with an educated guess, and then add or subtract in real time until your list becomes an indispensable tool to help increase the odds of success every time you use it.

Carry On
. . . .

When are you done refining your list? Never. (Sorry!) To quote Walmart founder Sam Walton, "To succeed in this world, you have to change all the time." The repetition of refinement is what sets SUPER individuals and organizations apart from their competition—both current and future. Review your most important checklists at least quarterly. Even incremental improvements in employee and customer experience can yield exponential increases in profits.

Perhaps the most famous proponent of checklists in modern times is Atul Gawande, author of the *New York Times* bestseller *The Checklist Manifesto*. In the book, Gawande, a trained surgeon, extols the power of a simple checklist to save lives and protect against the growing complexities that technology has introduced into virtually every field. If you're looking for your next read, I suggest adding it to your *list*.

◀◀ SUPERQUICK! REWIND ◀◀

By automating tasks, you free up your time to focus on your customers. Don't be afraid to admit that a process can work better without your direct involvement in every step.

For the tasks you can't automate, create checklists, and use them until the steps become automatic. Checklists are one of the most powerful productivity tools ever invented. Channel your inner Santa Claus. Make some lists and check them twice.

15

Everybody Talks

. . . .

There is no advertisement as powerful as
a positive reputation traveling fast.
BRIAN KOSLOW

F YOU'VE ever heard a kindergartener tell a joke, there's a good chance you didn't just hear the joke once. Kids have a knack for repeating the same joke eight times to the same audience and thinking it's *hilarious* every time. They lose no enthusiasm with each retelling.

How convenient would it be if you could take a set-it-and-forget-it approach to creating superfans? Unfortunately, like exercise and sleeping, creating superfans is something you've got to make a daily practice if you want to see results. If you can muster the same enthusiasm as a six-year-old telling a knock-knock joke, even better. Hence the final pillar of the SUPER Model: repeat.

Over and Over
. . . .

We're all creatures of habit. We like to know what to expect. That's why franchises are so popular. There's comfort in the fact that, anywhere in the world, a Big Mac is going to taste pretty much the same. Looking for an assortment of random items in an unfamiliar town at 11 p.m.? There's probably a Walmart a few miles away, and the store layout is going to be nearly identical to the one in your hometown.

What about when things *aren't* how we're expecting them to be, or when they change from experience to experience? Let's say you try a new restaurant with your spouse. The chicken parm is *amazing*, so you both go back the next week. You order the same entrees, but they're only so-so. You don't know which experience was the exception. Do you roll the dice and try a third time? Maybe. Maybe not.

Repetition is critical for amazing customer experience. Jesse Cole is the owner of the baseball team the Savannah Bananas. They're known for wacky and fun experiences at their ballpark, including choreographed player dances and in-game skits. As Jesse likes to say, *every* game is someone's first game. Major league franchises are often great at planning fan experiences for opening day and the playoffs, but the Bananas aim to make every game feel that special because, to someone in the stands, it is. Bananas home games have been sold out for years. The team has earned a reputation for fun by repeatedly showcasing their uniqueness, game after game. Fans buy season tickets and come back again and again because they *know* they'll have a great time.

Our actions teach our customers what to expect. And because sharing feedback about experiences has never been quicker or easier, those actions reach far beyond the customers who are immediately impacted.

Somebody Told Me
. . . .

Decades ago, if you wanted the scoop on a business you'd never worked with, you had to ask around or depend on things like newspaper and magazine reviews, Michelin guides, or segments on local TV news programs. These days, there are dozens of websites customers can call up instantly to get an idea about what people are saying.

Depending on your business, sites and search engines like Google, Yelp, Trustpilot, Facebook, BBB, Angi, and Tripadvisor can make or break your chances of converting new prospects into customers. Yet, far too many businesses treat the all-important role of reputation management as an afterthought. Whether you're B2B, B2C, or B2B2C, your customers are going to talk. Your job is to monitor the conversation and, to the extent you can do so, influence it in your favor.

When I say "influence," I don't mean trying to game the system. Nearly everyone has been burned by purchasing a product with amazing 5-star reviews, only to find it was terrible. Sites are cracking down on reviews that were purchased or collected as part of promotions, but far too many businesses try to take the easy way out and pay for fake reviews.

Don't say, "Can you please leave me a 5-star review?" Instead, ask your satisfied customers to leave *honest* feedback. You can say (or write) something like: "One of the ways we keep our prices reasonable is by not spending money on advertising. Instead, we ask our amazing customers to help spread the word. If [whatever your thing is] exceeded your expectations, please don't keep it to yourself! Telling your friends or leaving a quick, honest review on [insert two places *max*—one is better] will help even more great people like you find us."

Many parts of your reputation management program can be automated to help amplify both your collection of qualified feedback and your online presence. Emails asking for feedback and/or referrals should be on your "after" checklist and integrated into your process for all customers.

Both public and private feedback are valuable, and successful businesses put systems in place for collecting and responding to both. Just don't make it a painful task for your customers. I recently received a survey from an airline about a flight. After more than a dozen questions asking me about everything from the cleanliness of the airport bathroom to the wait at the boarding gate, I noticed the little progress bar at the bottom of the screen was only at 40 percent. I immediately bailed. A survey about a flight shouldn't be longer than the flight.

Whataya Want from Me

By being intentional about asking for things like reviews and referrals at the right time, you can amplify the impact of each experience.

Once, the head of marketing at an international charity asked me if I knew the number-one reason people gave for donating to her organization. I thought about it for a moment and said, "Is it because they suffered at some point in their past?"

Wrong. I tried again. "Because they're looking for a tax break, and they see the impact in their community?" Nope.

The executive told me that, time and time again, when the charity surveyed donors to ask why they had contributed, an overwhelming majority of people said it was *because someone asked them to donate.* They received a call to action. A phone call or letter in the mail or email that solicited a donation with a specific ask.

So powerful, and yet so simple. After she told me this, I began my own informal analysis of customers and clients. Overwhelmingly, customers told me they had left reviews because they were asked to do so. Clients who referred new business to me often did so because I asked for referrals.

Maya Angelou said, "Ask for what you want and be prepared to get it." Making specific, easy requests to delighted customers at the right moment is an incredibly low-cost way to boost your reputation and fill your pipeline with high-quality, warm leads via referrals.

If you're a B2C company, you might say something like: "If you know someone else who would love [your thing], we'd love an introduction! You can share the code [your offer code] and you'll both get [offer]."

B2B? Try this: "It's been so great working with you! Thanks again for everything. If you've got any colleagues who might be interested in [your thing], I would really appreciate an introduction—especially if they're as great as you! I'll make sure any friend you send this way gets white-glove treatment." Then, offer an email template or marketing materials to make it simple for the customer to tell their friends.

Looking for more ideas for increasing the number of referrals coming your way? You'll find several of my favorite scripts at BrittanyHodak.com/SUPER.

◄◄ SUPERQUICK! REWIND ◄◄

Repetition makes reputation and reputation makes customers. Reviews and referrals from delighted customers are an effective and low-cost way to multiply your revenue, so make it a practice to ask for them on a regular basis.

Knowledge comes by taking things apart... but wisdom comes by putting things together.

JOHN A. MORRISON

PART 7

SUPER-CHARGED: PUTTING IT ALL TOGETHER

16

Pet Sounds

. . . .

Always deliver more than expected.

LARRY PAGE

OW LONG does it take to turn a customer into a superfan? Sometimes it can happen in a matter of minutes. That was the case for me the first time I shopped with online pet retailer Chewy.com. I've shared stories about dozens of SUPER brands from the stage over the years. The brand that always sparks the most stories from audience members is Chewy. Everyone, it seems, has a Chewy story or knows someone who does. Even more impressive is the fact that many people can recall not just the SUPER experience they received, but also the name of the *employee* who wowed them.

The first Chewy employee who wowed me was named Kelly. It was about ten minutes after I placed my first-ever order on the site for prescription dog food for one of my dogs. The product page noted that a vet prescription was required to fill the order and should be submitted via email. Here's the email I sent to what I assumed was an automated inbox:

> Hello,
>
> Below and attached please find the Rx authorization for order number NCC1701.
>
> Thanks,
> BRITTANY

It was a Saturday, so I figured it would be Monday before I received any kind of human-aided response. Instead, a response came seven minutes later. It said:

> Hi there Brittany,
>
> Thanks so much for sending Bear's prescription directly. I've applied it to your order, and everything is set. Once it ships out, you'll get an email confirmation and a tracking number. If you need anything at all, give us a bark. We're here 24/7 to lend a helping paw.
>
> Chow-Chow for now,
> KELLY

That email elevates what could have been an ordinary, forgettable interaction into a memorable one. Let's break it down.

> Hi there Brittany,

Right off the bat, Kelly is friendly and conversational. Salutations matter because they set the tone for the rest of the communication.

> Thanks so much for sending Bear's prescription directly.

Kelly thanks me, and then she does something else. Something subtle, but important: she mentions Bear's name. I didn't mention Bear's name in my initial email, but she looked at the prescription and called him by name in her response. Why? Because Bear isn't just another faceless, nameless customer. He's not just an order number. He's *my* dog. In her response, Kelly is signaling that she cares about Bear, too.

> I've applied it to your order, and everything is set. Once it ships out, you'll get an email confirmation and a tracking number.

This was my first Chewy order, so Kelly's expectation setting is smart and helpful. She confirms that she's taken care of the immediate to-do (applying the prescription) and lets me know what to expect next. Most importantly, this assures me that there's nothing else for me to do. How many times have you received an email from a customer service rep and been unsure about what to expect next—or when to expect it? Kelly's note leaves no ambiguity: everything is set.

> If you need anything at all, give us a bark. We're here 24/7 to lend a helping paw.

Could Kelly have said "We work 24/7" and left it at that? Yes. Employees of many other organizations would have. Instead, Kelly connects her story to mine. She uses cute, fun dog puns that tell me at once that she and Chewy are friendly, approachable, and happy to help anytime I need them.

> Chow-Chow for now,
> KELLY

Another dog pun for the win! The email ends as strong as it started. Yes, the play on *ciao/chow* is cute. But the addition of "for now" is brilliant. She's not saying "bye" forever. She's saying bye "for now," with the assumption that we'll speak again. It's a subtle nod to the fact that this is now an ongoing relationship. Chewy—and Kelly—are there for me.

Finally, Kelly ends the email with her name. It doesn't say "Chewy team" or "Chewy customer service," because teams and departments don't send emails; people do.

The email is masterful. Chewy and Kelly didn't settle for "good enough"—they were *super*.

Would an automated email that said, "Hello, an Rx was received and will be applied to your order" have made the same impact? Of course not. Yet far too many businesses settle for okay. They've become fine with mundane. Instead of using touchpoints to tell stories and create superfans, they squander them by doing the bare minimum.

Writing good emails doesn't cost any more than writing bad emails. It doesn't even take that much longer. I'm sure Kelly (and the rest of her colleagues) use templates to respond to customers so quickly. But does it feel like a templated response when I receive it? No. It's helpful and funny and personable.

If the first email from Chewy impressed me, it's safe to say the next one knocked me off my feet. A few minutes after receiving Kelly's email, I typed out a quick reply from my iPhone:

> Perfect! Thanks so much for the quick response, Kelly. I really appreciate it—and so does Bear!
>
> Have a great day,
> BRITTANY

I wasn't expecting a reply; it just felt right to acknowledge the personal email she'd sent my way. To my surprise, Kelly wrote back. Almost immediately. She said:

> Hi there Brittany,
>
> Absolutely, it's our pleasure! We're so thankful every day for each and every wonderful member of our Chewy family, like you. Please tell

Bear we said hello—if you ever happen to snap a cute photo of him enjoying his Chewy goodies, feel free to send it our way. We always love meeting our VIPs (Very Important Paws).

We're here 24/7, 365 days a year, rain or shine—if you ever need a helping paw or a listening ear, simply bark in our direction! We're always happy to hear from you.

Over and snout,
KELLY

Another email, another masterclass.

So much goodness packed into 100 words. I'm not just a customer, I'm part of a *family*! Bear is a VIP—and one they want to meet! She doubles down on the 24/7 thing, making me believe she really *would* be happy to hear from me any time. Close it out with another dog pun, and it's over: I'm officially a Chewy superfan.

I went from awareness ("Oh yeah, I think I've heard of that website") to action ("I'll buy this dog food here") to advocacy ("Check out this email from Chewy—they're amazing!") in fifteen minutes flat. Why? Because Kelly connected *her* story ("I care about your pet, and I'm here to help!") to *my* story ("Great! I need help with my dog!"). She's catapulting Chewy from a commodity provider ("We sell dog food") to a category of one ("You're part of the family, and your pet is a VIP"). I don't care if Kelly and her colleagues sent very similar emails to a thousand other customers that day—it still felt special when she sent it to *me*.

I wrote back again, not because it was necessary, but because I *wanted* to. At this point, I felt like we knew each other. "Of course I have pictures of my pups!" I told her, offering up a link to Instagram. She responded to say how adorable they were, and how much she and her colleagues enjoyed flipping through the photos. That's the kind of connection that makes a customer come back *and* tell their friends.

I quickly began shifting purchases from other retailers to Chewy, ordering everything from toys to treats to flea and tick medicine on auto-ship. I was the receiving end of several "wow" interactions from Chewy relatively quickly.

Is This Love

About a week after I placed that first order, Bear got a handwritten "Welcome!" postcard in the mail. A few days later, I received a call from an employee who was getting in touch just to ask if the dog food had helped Bear recover from his GI issues. I said it had, and she suggested a few other non-prescription dog foods from the same line that might be a good choice going forward.

A few weeks later, a box arrived that I wasn't expecting. Inside was an assortment of toys and treats with a note from a Chewy employee named Allison, saying how much she'd enjoyed watching a video I'd posted online of my pups pawing at a Chewy box. I tagged Chewy in the cute video, but I never expected them to connect the dots from a social post back to my customer account in their CRM— and I certainly didn't expect them to send a box with goodies and a personalized note to Bear and his brother, Bandit.

I soon found out Kelly's 24/7 promise wasn't just talk. One night around 2 a.m., I walked downstairs to find Bear licking the oily, goopy flea and tick medicine I'd applied to Bandit a few hours earlier off his back. I immediately freaked out, worried that Bear was going to get sick. I woke up my husband, who suggested I call pet poison control. I said, "I'll start with Chewy. I bet they'll know what to do."

Sure enough, a friendly Chewy customer support employee picked up my call immediately and asked how she could help. I told her what happened, and she immediately went into triage mode, looking up the ingredients and suggesting what I do next.

Before the end of our call (and after reassuring me more than once that I wasn't a terrible pet parent), she said, "By the way, did you know there are chews you can give your dogs for flea and tick protection?"

I had no idea. I was simultaneously excited not to have to squeeze the little tube of goop onto squirming dogs' spines again and annoyed at my vet for not telling me such a medical marvel existed.

She said, "I see both Bandit and Bear are up to date on their vet visits. Would you like someone from our pharmacy to call your vet and get a prescription for the chews?"

I said yes without hesitation. I was *floored* by the next words out of her mouth: "I also see you still have a few months' worth of the liquid flea and tick medicine that you ordered last month. I'm going to refund your credit card for that purchase. Feel free to donate the unopened doses to your favorite shelter or rescue organization."

At the time, I'd spent a few hundred dollars at Chewy. Some brands might look at that and think, "She is not a priority customer. Don't go out of your way." Instead, Chewy recognizes the potential lifetime value of each customer. Now, nearly six years after my first Chewy order, I've spent several thousand dollars, and continue to spend money each month on food, treats, and preventative medications that auto-ship without me ever having to think about it.

A couple of years after my first purchase, another surprise arrived from Chewy: hand-painted canvas portraits of Bandit and Bear. I was so excited that I immediately hung them on the wall—and, of course, shared them on social media. Nearly every time someone comes to my house for the first time, they look at the portraits (which now hang in

WHEN YOU SAY

★ ★ ★ YOU'RE GREAT, ★ ★ ★

IT'S MARKETING

WHEN OTHER PEOPLE SAY

★ ★ ★ YOU'RE GREAT, ★ ★ ★

IT'S MAGIC

our entryway) and say something like, "Oh, wow. Did you get pictures painted of your dogs?" Each time I get to say, "No, Chewy sent those to us!" and tell the story all over again.

When you say that you're great, it's marketing. When *other* people say that you're great, it's magic. Be so exceptional that it forces your customers to talk about you.

I love talking about Chewy during keynotes because in every audience, whether it's twenty people or two thousand, someone has a Chewy story to share with me. At least a dozen people have told me about Chewy sending flowers after the loss of their pet. One customer told me Chewy had refunded his credit card for a purchase of more than $1,000 for super-pricey medicine after his cat passed away. Countless people have told me about receiving toys and treats (and sometimes even clothes) for their pets unannounced, always accompanied by a sweet note from a member of the Chewy team.

Chewy stories like these go viral on a shockingly consistent basis. At least once a month someone who has seen me speak onstage sends me a link to a social post about a Chewy act of kindness that had a profound impact on a customer. I don't know of any other brand that goes viral for amazing CX with the regularity of Chewy.

Simply the Best

Chewy has mastered personalization at scale to surprise and delight their customers. The business was founded in 2011 with CX at its core. In its first year, Chewy did about $26 million in sales. Just six years later, the company had captured a 51 percent market share of online pet food sales in the U.S., and had grown to approximately $2 billion in annual sales. That year, Chewy was acquired by PetSmart for $3.35 billion. At the time, it was the largest-ever e-commerce business acquisition—in a category where PetSmart had been operating for decades before Chewy existed. PetSmart later spun off the brand and, in 2019, Chewy IPO'd at a valuation of more than $10 billion. A relentless obsession with customer experience *works*. Chewy and its employees embody what it means to be SUPER. Now let's break down how.

S | Start with your story

Every Chewy employee is a pet lover. It's a prerequisite to getting the gig. Whether they're in customer service, logistics, product development, or anything in between, they love pets. That creates an easy starting point to connect with Chewy's mission of supporting pets and their people.

U | Understand your customer's story

Chewy employees know that customers love their pets and want what's best for them. They also know that they're likely to interact with pet parents who are dealing with stressful situations: for example, a new kitten or a sick bunny. There is *always* empathy in customer interactions.

P | Personalize

Chewy employees know that *my* pets are the most important pets in the world to me. They also know that messages about hamsters and fish and cats aren't relevant to me, so their marketing team doesn't talk to me about those things.

E | Exceed expectations

Chewy employees do what it takes to elevate interactions into experiences, which is why there are thousands of examples of posts about Chewy employees' actions going viral.

You know who doesn't garner worldwide acclaim on a regular basis for delighting customers? Every other player in the pet industry. Chewy dominates this area, which is part of the reason their customers are so incredibly loyal.

R | Repeat

Chewy has created numerous systems to help guarantee that every interaction is a wow. Their team has repeatedly looked for ways to improve *every* part of the customer experience, for *every* customer.

Here's just one example of how Chewy looks for ways to create wow. You know how when you call most businesses you hear a pre-recorded message that says something like, "This call may be recorded for quality assurance and training purposes"? Well, you don't hear that when you call Chewy's support number. Why? Because they don't want to keep customers waiting for the extra 1.5 seconds it takes to hear that message. They want to connect callers with a human as quickly as possible.

The other implication of that decision is that, unlike most call centers, Chewy doesn't record calls, since in many states it's illegal to record calls without announcing that fact. But Chewy executives don't care. They trust their employees and the training they receive. There's no need to record calls "for quality assurance" when you've built a culture where quality is the point of entry, not the lofty goal.

Never Gonna Give You Up

Everything in the breakdown you just read is based on my own personal experiences with the brand. Now, here's some language in the company's own words, excerpted from Chewy's Investor Relations site.

CORPORATE OVERVIEW

Our mission is to be the most trusted and convenient destination for pet parents (and partners) everywhere. We view pets (and pet parents) as family and are obsessed with meeting their needs and exceeding customer expectations through every interaction.

Launched in 2011, we offer the personalized service of a neighborhood pet store alongside the convenience and speed of e-commerce . . .

Chewy's commitment to customer service is the core of our brand, and our customers love us for it. We "WOW" pet parents through 24/7 assistance, advice and encouragement every day of the year . . .

As an e-commerce company, product innovation drives our operations, and our team is constantly striving to find new and better ways to improve our customers' experience.

Sounds SUPER familiar, right?

Chewy ended its 2021 fiscal year with $8.9 billion in net sales, 20.7 million active customers, and more than 21,000 team members. That's the kind of business it's possible to build when a company commits to creating superfans.

At every turn, Chewy could have made the choice to be average, as so many companies do. Sometimes it only takes the voice of a few leaders who don't value being SUPER to make the kind of short-sighted decisions that keep so many companies in the pack with their commonplace competitors. It's not hard to imagine someone questioning the choices Chewy made that are now, in hindsight, the building blocks of its identity.

Chewy could've made the decision to just send welcome emails instead of personalized, handwritten cards. "It will be much cheaper, and it's still a nice way to greet customers," someone might've said in a budget meeting once upon a time. Emails would've been easier, too, but Chewy didn't choose the easy path.

They could've made the choice to use chatbots, or to outsource to a call center to field their customer inquiries. "That's what our competitors are doing, anyway," an internal naysayer might've argued. But Chewy didn't settle for average.

"Sending out personalized portraits of tens of thousands of pets? Really? Show me the ROI!" someone might've shouted.

"We don't need to wow them every time. It's pet food! We just need to be a little bit better than the other guys," this imaginary supervillain might've mused. "Free, fast shipping? Absolutely not. Charge for it!"

Every company gets to choose what it wants for its customers. Chewy could've chosen the common path. Instead, again and again, they make the choice to be SUPER, and it's made all the difference.

Let someone else be average. Your customers are craving *more*.

Treat every customer like an influencer and you will be rewarded with loyalty and lifetime value beyond your wildest imagination. Align your team around this all-important cause and your entire pack will be creating tail-wagging superfans in no time.

◄◄ SUPERQUICK! REWIND ◄◄

Chewy's mission "to be the most trusted and convenient destination for pet parents (and partners) everywhere" informs every decision the company makes. Their obsession with customers helped the brand go from startup to multi-billion-dollar IPO in under a decade.

If people can be passionate about where they order pet food and medications, you can make your customers passionate about whatever you're doing, one SUPER experience at a time.

17

Come as You Are

. . . .

Already know you, that which you need.
YODA

MY OLDEST SON, Kadoh, is a Star Wars superfan. From the time he wakes up to the time he goes to sleep, it's all Star Wars, all the time. One of his favorite stories is a Little Golden Book called *I Am a Jedi*. I've read it to him countless times, and it always makes me think about customer experience—and not just because of a certain Wookiee whose nickname rhymes with "gooey."

There's an illustration of Yoda and Obi-Wan Kenobi alongside the words, "Some Jedi are big. Some Jedi are small. Size matters not." If you read the Chewy story in the last chapter and thought, "That's great for them, but I don't have 20,000 employees and billions of dollars," don't despair. Just like with the Force, the greatest wielders of SUPER powers know that size is irrelevant.

Whether you've got one employee or 1 million, an unwavering focus on customers will elevate your brand and help you earn both repeat and referral business, as a clothing retailer in my town knows all too well.

Good Vibrations

. . . .

Nashville and its surrounding suburbs are filled with boutique cloth-
ing stores. While many of them blur together, one of my favorites,
Finnleys, firmly stands out. Their motto, "Pretty things. Great people.
Good vibes," is exactly what you'll find if you visit any of their stores.

I want to pause for a moment and acknowledge the brilliance
of that motto. The best mottos are shortened versions of a brand's
story, and this one is no exception. In six words, Finnleys tells you
everything you need to know about its products, its employees, and
how its experience will make you feel. Six words! The shop, which
has grown to three locations since founder Dawn Craig launched the
first store in downtown Franklin, Tennessee, in 2014, firmly checks
every SUPER box.

S | Start with your story

Great origin story? Check. This is directly from the Finnleys website:

> Since starting this business . . . Finnleys has been inspired by my
> daughter Finnley, from our name to our mission. Finnley has a con-
> fident sense of self I hope all women can feel, which is why we call
> ourselves Finnleys—plural, not possessive.

U | Understand your customer's story

Here's another passage from the website that proves Finnleys understands exactly what its customers are looking for. Spoiler alert: it isn't
just clothes.

> Finnleys helps our customers define their confident sense of self,
> offering a wide selection of expressive, trendy fashion pieces.
>
> Our stores offer a fun, relaxed shopping environment with stylists
> who want to help you find pieces reflective of you and your personality.

THE BEST
★ MOTTOS ★

———— ARE ————

SHORTENED VERSIONS

———— OF A ————

BRAND'S STORY

P | Personalize

As a longtime Finnleys shopper, I know that sales associates go out of their way to connect with every customer, making the phrase "We can't wait to meet you!" on their site and socials ring true.

On a recent trip I took to a Finnleys location in Nashville's 12 South neighborhood, a stylist named Meg told me the best part of her job was that new accessories and clothing arrive every week. "It means I'm always helping our customers find new things!" she said with genuine excitement.

Finnleys doesn't simply connect with their customers in stores, either. From birthday discounts to fun surprise offers and shout-outs, they're masters at keeping customers engaged in their inboxes and on social media.

E | Exceed expectations

Back to the Finnleys website one last time:

> Our stores are designed to yield nothing but enjoyable experiences where people leave feeling encouraged and inspired. We want you to find pieces that reflect YOUR unique personality, and our stylists are here to make that mission come to life.

People can find cute clothes anywhere. At one Finnleys store, customers are greeted by an Instagram-ready photo wall that features lush greenery, shiny disco balls, and a hot pink neon sign that reads, "Hello, Gorgeous!"

At another location, bachelorette parties wait around the block to pose alongside a mural on the store's brick facade. Giant candy hearts emblazoned with phrases like "What Would Dolly Do?" and "Cheers Y'all" and "Let's Go Girls" brighten the bricks like polka dots. It's not just a clothing store; it's a destination.

R | .Repeat

Why do Finnleys customers keep coming back? It's not just for the fun photo ops and the ever-rotating slate of merchandise. It's because they leave feeling great, even if they don't buy anything.

Don't Stop Believin'
. . . .

Your own "Pretty things. Great people. Good vibes" might look and sound completely different. After all, every superpower is unique. Find yours and don't stop until you're the best in the world at it because, as Yoda might say, "Also SUPER, you can be."

A Jedi in training is called a Padawan. Padawans must be taught the ways of the Force before becoming a Jedi Knight. You've now been trained in the ways of Superfandom, one of the most powerful forces in the universe. The next section of this book applies the SUPER Model to various roles and departments to help accelerate and amplify its company-wide application. Every company, large and small, can use the SUPER Model framework to build a reputation as a category leader.

Size matters not, and your path, you must decide. Make the choice to be SUPER, and the Force will be with you. Always.

◄◄ SUPERQUICK! REWIND ◄◄

When it comes to creating SUPER experiences, size is not a limitation. If you want to design experiences that your customers will tell their friends about and come back to experience again, you are bound only by your creativity.

Find a group of people who
challenge and inspire you,
spend a lot of time with them,
and it will change your life.

AMY POEHLER

SUPER-
GROUPS:
BREAKDOWN

18

Ain't No Stoppin' Us Now

SUPER TEAMS

· · · · · · · · · · · · · · · · · ·

Individuals don't win in business. Teams do.

SAM WALTON

E MPLOYEE EXPERIENCE, or EX, is at the heart of all CX. It is exceedingly unlikely that employees will treat customers better than they are treated. If you truly want to create a culture of superfandom, you've got to start by treating your employees like the critical component of success they are.

What's the cost of a single disengaged employee? While it's hard to quantify, it can sometimes stretch to ten figures. In 2017, superstar writer and director Shonda Rhimes was producing nearly seventy hours of content for ABC that was responsible for more than $2 billion in ad revenue, according to the *Hollywood Reporter*. However, she was unhappy with what felt to her like near-constant pushback from the network.

The breaking point in her longtime relationship with ABC and parent company Disney came when a network executive gave her a hard time about getting an all-inclusive pass to Disneyland for a family member.

When she made the request, she was told multiple times "We never do this." Finally, the network gave her an extra pass, but for some reason, it didn't work correctly when it was scanned at the park's entrance.

Rhimes called a high-ranking exec, assuming he could fix the issue. Instead, he reportedly replied, "Don't you have enough?" Rhimes was polite, but when she hung up, she immediately called her representatives and instructed them to get her a deal somewhere else.

What followed was a nine-figure deal at Netflix and a huge hole at ABC. The network lost one of the most successful creators in its history because executives weren't willing to help someone responsible for $2 *billion* in ad revenue get a Disneyland pass.

Could Rhimes have afforded her own pass? Of course. But it wasn't about the pass. It was about what the pass represented. Rhimes, who was contributing enormously to the company's bottom line, felt disrespected and unappreciated, so she found a job elsewhere.

While the primary purpose of this book is to help turn customers into superfans, the model for creating superfan employees is exactly the same. And, once you've got a team full of superfans *inside* the company, your superfan customers will multiply exponentially.

We Are the Champions

Disney has "cast members," Starbucks has "partners," Chewy has "Chewtopians," and Target has "team members."

Having a term (or terms) for your teammates is a touchpoint where you can share something about your culture and remind employees of the larger role they're playing.

Brand manager Alix Steinberg learned this as a teenager when she was a counselor at a YMCA camp in Massachusetts. Like most counselors, Alix and her peers wore brightly colored shirts to help children and parents identify them. However, the shirts didn't say "STAFF"—they said "ROLE MODEL."

"During our orientation at the start of each summer, the camp directors made it a point to call us 'role models' instead of staff or counselors," Alix said. "They reminded us that campers are *always* watching and empowered us to set an example and instill the camp's four core values of Caring, Honesty, Respect, and Responsibility every day."

She was only seventeen when she started as a counselor, but Alix returned to work at the camp for five more summers. "I loved wearing that shirt," she said. "When I put it on every morning, I felt inspired to lead my campers. Other camps had 'staff' that supervised campers as they played games, but *I* was a 'role model.' I didn't just watch over kids as they swam—I helped shape the character of each child and make a positive impact on their development. I will always be proud of the six summers I spent as a YMCA camp role model. It's amazing the power a title can have."

Teammate names are just the beginning. Here are other examples of how the SUPER Model can elevate your employee experience.

S | Start with your story

Why does the company exist? Is there alignment between your stated mission, vision, and values and the way you treat your employees?

Ensure that every employee not only understands your company's story but also how *they* fit into it. As I've said over and over, every single employee at your company can make or break a customer's experience.

The employee onboarding process should familiarize every new hire with the company's story. They should be able to internalize it and share a version of it by the end of their orientation. More importantly, they should be able to explain why *they* chose to work at the company through the lens of that story. Their reason might not rise to the level of a calling, but it should absolutely be more compelling than "I needed a job."

If an employee doesn't feel connected to the company's story, it will never be more than a job to them. There's no problem too small to be important if it's framed in the right way. And, when you frame an opportunity correctly, you'll attract the right team members.

Trader Joe's VP of marketing, Matt Sloan, broke down the brand's reputation for friendly employees in an episode of the company's podcast. He explained that the chain hires nice people and treats them well, which makes them happier. What a concept, right? "It turns out taking care of our crew is good business," he said.

Trader Joe's has been able to replicate its culture again and again, store after store, with crew members who care about the store, its unique products, and its local customers. Your company's story must invoke a sense of purpose and pride in your employees.

You can begin sharing your company's uniqueness even before the application process begins. Here are a few headlines from different company career pages that send a message to would-be applicants considering jobs with their brands:

- **Amazon:** Come build the future with us.
- **Associated Press (AP):** Join us in telling the world's story.
- **Crate & Barrel:** We have everything we need to inspire our customers. Except you.
- **LEGO:** Come and play.

- **Little Caesars:** We serve more than pizza. We serve people.
- **Party City:** Join the party!
- **Publix:** You'd look good in green.
- **Ulta:** The possibilities are beautiful.

What do you think—would you want to work at any of these companies?

Imagine you're trying to decide which company to apply at. Whether it's your first job or your fifteenth—the headlines above are going to grab your attention more than "Careers" or "Search for an Opening" or "We're Hiring" or "Jobs Hub," all of which are real examples pulled directly from competitors of businesses in the examples I just listed. Words like "Come" and "Join" are inviting prospective applicants *into the story* of the brands before they've even applied.

Everything is experience, and every touchpoint is an opportunity to begin telling your brand's story. Attracting the right members to join your team is a critical part of building a SUPER brand. After all, it's not always the team with the best play calling or the best coaching that makes it to the Super Bowl—you've got to have terrific players in the right positions, too.

U | Understand your employees' stories

Engaged employees are, of course, a huge competitive advantage for businesses, and the same techniques that apply to customers—active listening, empathy and authority, asking for regular feedback, and so on—are true for employees as well. Everyone wants to feel appreciated and receive validation. They want to know that their STORY matters to their boss, their boss's boss, and their boss's boss's boss.

Every business needs a VoE (Voice of Employee) program that regularly collects feedback from employees. Capturing—and, more importantly, *acting on*—regular feedback from employees not only helps you better understand your team, it also improves employee retention. Survey your employees at least twice a year. Once per quarter is even better. You may choose to make one survey anonymous and the next on the record, as there are benefits to both.

Finding and training new employees is so much harder and more expensive than retaining good ones, just as selling to new customers is costlier and more difficult than retaining existing ones.

Diversity, equity, and inclusion are also key parts of creating well-functioning teams. Your entire company—from the boardroom to the break room—should feature representation from as diverse a population as your prospective customer base includes. For more best practices, visit BrittanyHodak.com/SUPER.

P | Personalize

Where are superfan employees created? Say it with me: *at the intersection of your story and every customer's story.* Personalization is paramount to keeping great employees aligned and engaged. One example that's becoming more and more meaningful to employees is workplace independence. Giving team members the ability to work wherever—and often whenever—they want can mean the difference in getting the best candidate for a job versus getting the best candidate in your zip code with availability on weekdays from 8 to 5.

The Platinum Rule is as critical for interacting with employees as it is for customers. To the extent that you can personalize your approach to your colleagues, do so. Little things like using a preferred method of contact ("Do you prefer Slack messages or a quick phone call?") can go a long way toward showing someone on your team that you care about their preferences.

— EVERY —
TOUCHPOINT
★ ★ ★ ★ ★ IS AN ★ ★ ★ ★ ★
OPPORTUNITY
— TO TELL —
YOUR BRAND'S
— STORY —

E | Exceed expectations

Just as a customer's perception of your company is taking shape well before they ever make a purchase, you're offering cues to future potential employees long before they fill out an application. You can exceed expectations by mapping all the moments that matter and elevating them into memorable experiences.

Think about the common struggles of a new job and alleviate as many as possible before they occur. Things like having an easily accessible org chart with photos and contact info, a one-page overview of the company's story, or a how-to guide for necessary hardware or software not only help new team members find their footing, but they also eliminate the need to solve repetitive issues again and again. Talk to a few recently onboarded team members and ask for their honest feedback on what would've made the experience even easier.

Going beyond what's expected to take care of your employees will teach them to go above and beyond for customers. In addition to the gifting best practices you learned in Chapter 10, here are a few ways you can show your employees how much you care:

- Before a new employee begins, send a custom "Welcome!" box with branded swag and items that reflect your company's culture and unique story. You can even customize it for each new hire and their family: a onesie for the newborn ("My mommy works at Acme!"), a dish for the family dog, and so on. You can customize welcome boxes further if you capture information about favorite things, like restaurants, sports teams, or treats.

- Early in a new employee's journey, collect information about their growth goals so managers can help with both personal and professional development.

- Offer company-wide wellness days/weeks, where everyone in the company has time off to relax or reflect.

- Consider giving every employee a small monthly allocation to spend on anything they'd like: books, music streaming services, concert tickets, etc.—anything to help them take care of themselves.

R | Repeat

Anyone who's ever built a team knows that reputation is even more important to potential employees than it is to customers. While customers give you their money, employees give you something far, far more valuable: their time and their talents.

The more systems and processes you create to ensure predictably positive outcomes for your employees, the better your reputation will be—and the easier it will be to recruit new prospects to join the team. Use the "before, during, and after" approach in Chapter 11 to map employee journeys, and then create checklists for your managers to use at every critical juncture.

SUPER companies know that if they put people before profits, profits *will* follow. Conversely, prioritizing profits will not always lead to world-class people. You can have both, but you must do it in the right order. People first. Always.

◀◀ SUPERQUICK! REWIND ◀◀

Your team is the heart of your brand. If you don't have superfans inside your company, it's virtually impossible to have them outside your company. Treat your employees so well that they can't imagine leaving.

With a Little Help from My Friends

SUPER SOCIAL MEDIA

. . . .

Do not... address your readers as though they were gathered together in a stadium. When people read your copy, they are alone. Pretend you are writing to each of them a letter.
DAVID OGILVY

ONE TOPIC I'm frequently asked about at speaking engagements is social media. Many professionals have told me they find social media intimidating, believing they're "too old" or "too uncool" to keep up with an ever-growing slate of new networks and trends, each with its own nuances and norms. Others are uncomfortable about the privacy implications of this experiment we're all living through.

Others simply don't see the need to incorporate social media into their businesses. "I've been selling insurance for thirty years without social media. I see no reason to change now," someone told me once. My answer, by the way, was this: You're not selling insurance to people thirty years ago—you're selling insurance today. If you don't want to reach new customers via social media, that's fine! Someone else will be more than happy to take that business from you.

Forget "followers." You're not a cult leader (at least I hope you're not!). Focus on fans: the people who are excited by you and whatever it is that you do.

This chapter is about using social media to connect your story to your customer's story in a way that feels natural and authentic to you. These tactics will work for whatever sites and apps you're on now, as well as those that haven't been invented yet. That's because the art of connecting your story to your customer's story has been around for millennia and will outlast all of the networks we're using to tell our stories at this moment in time—and it will outlast all of us, too.

Name of the Game

The two keys to success on any social platform, current or future, are right there in the name: Social and Media. Sneaky, right? It's so obvious, yet tons of people never quite focus on either of those aspects of any new network they join.

First: Social. To find success on any platform, you've got to be social. Remember how much effort it used to take to make a long-distance phone call? Or mail a postcard? Billions of people are online. You can connect with them almost effortlessly, immediately, and for pennies. Do it!

Next: Media. Your social media channels are media that *you* curate and control. Imagine yourself as the head of programming for a television network. What would you choose to put on the air, knowing that the collective programming choices will define your network's reputation and identity? Social networks are similar. Treat them as if you're curating your own personal network. The choices you make say something about you and the types of people you're hoping to attract.

With those two guiding principles in mind, here's how you can use SUPER to reach new heights with your social media game.

S | Start with your story

The most common mistake that I see professionals and entrepreneurs make with their social media—by *far*—is not having a strategy that guides the creation and distribution of the content they share. Instead, they just sort of follow trends, chase hashtags, or try to replicate what they see working for others.

As a result, they never establish a clear identity. Their personal brands are confusing or muddled. It's like those cable channels you kind of recognize but couldn't say for sure what they're all about or how they're different from the other 150 choices in the lineup with similar-sounding names.

A clear strategy helps you determine what is (and what is *not*) in alignment with your story. It gives you the confidence to create and share content that will connect with those in need of your expertise. It also helps you avoid feeling like you have to constantly reinvent your online brand to "fit in" with what others are doing.

Use your story as a North Star of sorts to guide the creation of your content and the curation of what you share. Think back to your Story Setlist from Chapter 6. What are the memorable things you can post about to increase the odds of connecting and staying top of mind with your target audience?

Both your original content and the curated content you share serve the same purpose: overpowering apathy. In social speak, it's called scroll-stopping. You've got to be compelling enough to get someone to literally stop scrolling and engage with your content.

You must (literally!) make them care, and a compelling story is the most powerful way to do it.

U | Understand your customer's story

Which social networks do you need to be active on? The ones where your customers and prospects are. If you don't have a presence on a particular network, it makes it harder for customers to refer you.

Depending on your customer base, it may be important for you to have a presence on every network. More likely, though, one or two will be disproportionally key.

Keep your ideal customer's STORY in mind when you create and share content. Are you speaking to the transformation they hope to undergo? Can you share information to help position you as the best option? You know where superfans are created; don't forget about their story!

P | Personalize

Social media is one of the fastest and most cost-effective ways to stay connected with customers and, in the process, meet new prospects. Remember, one of the keys is to be *social*. That doesn't just mean on *your* page. Engage with your customers. Leave comments on posts when they're celebrating a life milestone, asking for recommendations, or sharing a fun photo. Set aside time in your calendar every day just to catch up on what's happening in your most important customers' lives. Superfandom is a two-way street. You're more likely to be top of mind with them when you show that they're top of mind for you.

E | Exceed expectations

Social media is a great tool to help you exceed customer expectations. If a customer posts that she just ran her first marathon, don't just like the picture. Surprise her with a "recovery" massage and a pedicure, or something else you know she'd enjoy. Don't just write "Happy Birthday!" in a DM; use the social reminders of birthdays (which *should* be in your CRM already...) to make a donation to a client's favorite charity or to send a thoughtful gift.

You don't need production value to blow someone away in a video or a post—just knowledge and creativity. Show or teach them more than they were expecting and they'll not only remember, they'll also be more likely to share your name (or share your post!) when an opportunity arises.

R | Repeat

Rome wasn't built in a day, and your personal brand won't be, either. Consistency is key on social media. Don't commit to a weekly live series and give up after six weeks because you get "too busy." Don't jump from trend to trend so quickly that you give people digital whiplash. Make a plan and stick to it. The proverbial social media hares may seem flashier in the moment, but the tortoises are always the ones who win in the end.

◀◀ SUPERQUICK! REWIND ◀◀

Social media is a *super* way to connect with prospects and customers. The key to social media success is right there in the name:

SOCIAL: Always post with your audience in mind. Respond to your customer's questions or concerns and leave thoughtful comments to show them that you care.

MEDIA: Your social feeds are a curation of your brand identity. How do you want to be positioned in your customers' minds?

20

Show Me What You Got

SUPER MARKETING

. . . .

The future of marketing isn't big data,
it's big understanding.
JAY BAER

"**M**ARKETING" HAS become something of a catch-all term over the past fifteen years as social media and smartphones have become ubiquitous. It's no longer just about driving brand awareness and purchase intent—now, marketing departments are increasingly charged with tasks like online reputation, social media interactions, product and process innovation, communication automation (both internally and externally), management of events and activations, and much more.

Love Story
. . . .

The marketing department's impact is felt across all aspects of a business and at all stages of a customer's journey, beginning with a powerful brand story. Without that powerful, cohesive story—one that helps inform all decisions, inside and out—few companies break through the "commodity" wall to represent anything unique or differentiated, to customers or to employees. While each pillar of the SUPER Model has practical applications for marketing, perhaps none is more critical than the first.

S | Start with your story

Why does your brand exist? How is it actively improving the lives of your customers?

That question should guide every story your brand tells: your mission statement, your values statement, your vision statement, your purpose statement—everything.

You will, of course, tell several variations of your story for different audiences: customers, employees, investors, reporters, partners, suppliers, and so on. Unless all of those stories are rooted in explaining why your brand exists and how it serves your customers, you'll never achieve alignment. Without alignment, it's that much harder for your brand to become memorable. You might be part of the consideration set, but you're very unlikely to reach "category of one" status.

If you can't succinctly and confidently explain what problem(s) you solve—or, put even more plainly, the reason you exist—your employees won't understand either. And if they don't know, your customers don't have a shot. Your brand's mission statement shouldn't just be a poster on the wall no one looks at—it has to be a story that people are inspired by and feel as if they're a part of.

I was recently picking up lunch in the Chick-fil-A drive-through line and overheard one young employee say to another, "Those people at Taco Bell could never do what we do!" Her colleague answered back, "You're so right—they never could."

As one of the teenagers handed me my Icedream cone I said, "You're right, another restaurant could never replicate what you guys are doing here." She immediately looked embarrassed that I'd heard their conversation. I said, "Don't be embarrassed—own it! You're doing an amazing job. Thank you for making this and every experience remarkable." She smiled, answered with the common Chick-fil-A refrain, "My pleasure," and told me to have a wonderful day.

U | Understand your customer's story

I've written at length throughout this book about understanding customer stories. Regardless of where in the purchase funnel a prospect or lead falls, understanding their story is paramount to advancing the journey. Use the STORY framework in Chapter 7 and the SUPER Map in Chapter 11 to help you reach your goals.

P | Personalize

Personalization will continue to grow in importance in every sector and across every interaction customers have with brands. Each of us has a strong, innate desire to be treated as an individual, whether that's in the marketing copy that shows up in our inbox or the products being shown to us on our favorite website.

Personalizing every part of your marketing takes a bit longer and costs a bit more, but the results it will yield when done correctly are more than worth it. Remember: Superfandom is a two-way street. Show your customers that you care about them as individuals and they'll take notice . . . and they'll likely even return the favor.

E | Exceed expectations

I've said repeatedly that everything is experience, and experience is everything. But experience is also every*where*. It's every*one*. Your brand is like a giant puzzle, and every piece contributes to the big picture—even the small ones.

It's been my experience that a lot of "idea people" end up in the marketing department. It was true of me, and it's been true of hundreds of amazing marketers I've gotten to know over the years. If you're that dreamer or that big idea person on your team, listen to your gut. Don't let your enthusiasm be tamped down by the more pragmatic members on your team. Fight the good fight when you're making the case to go the extra mile or to put in the extra effort. Your prospects and customers will appreciate it. Details matter. The most beloved, most customer-centric brands in the world don't settle for good enough, and you shouldn't either.

R | Repeat

How long, and how often, can your brand repeat a tagline, slogan, or story? For as long as it works. Smokey the Bear has been teaching that "only you can prevent forest fires" since 1947. Many colleges' rally cries date back more than a century. According to *Adweek*, Allstate's "You're in good hands" slogan was born in 1950 when a sales manager's wife said that their ill daughter was "in good hands" with the doctor. The manager repeated that phrase at a company meeting, and a new advertising campaign was born.

Here, There and Everywhere

SUPER can be deployed for just about every other marketing function as well. If you're working in PR, understanding your story (an irresistible pitch) and your "customer" (for example, a reporter, blogger, or producer) is critical for success. If your pitch doesn't address something their readers are *struggling* with or a *transformation* they care about, they have several other *options* to address their *reservations*. Make it clear that *you* are the best choice because of your irresistible story.

Planning an event? SUPER is the perfect checklist for ensuring it's a memorable experience people will be excited to return to next year: What makes this event different (S) and how are you communicating that ahead of the event? Why does that matter to attendees (U)? How do you make everyone feel like a VIP (P) throughout the process? How will you exceed their expectations (E) at every turn? Are you making it easy for them to say "yes!" to coming back next year, even before this event ends (R)?

The same goes for advertising: start with a story people will want to retell by making it ring true to their experiences. Exceed their expectations (with humor or wisdom or anything else), and, when it works, repeat.

One of the most transformational things any marketing leader can do is help everyone in your company to be SUPER. This shared framework can improve every department without raising costs or requiring months of training. Lead by example with SUPER in your marketing efforts, and your company will create superfans.

◀◀ SUPERQUICK! REWIND ◀◀

Adapting SUPER can help your marketing team achieve its goals by aligning your brand's story with your customer's story, personalizing the content, exceeding expectations through humor or wisdom, and repeating your messaging until your customers know it by heart.

21

Money, Money, Money

SUPER SALES

. . . .

Make a customer, not a sale.

KATHERINE BARCHETTI

WAS WALKING through a mall in Las Vegas recently when I accidentally made eye contact with a mall-cart vendor. Big mistake. Before
I could avert my gaze, she said, "Wow, you're so pretty." I was flat-
tered, but before I could say "thank you," she finished what was
apparently a two-part thought: ". . . for someone with so much sun
damage on her face."

I stood in silence, thinking how quickly that took a turn. As I was processing her qualifier, she continued: "Give me fifteen minutes and I can
show you how to erase fifteen years of that discoloration and damage."

I was still confused. I asked, "Are you talking about my freckles?"
She answered, "After you turn thirty, they're not freckles. They're
sunspots. They aren't cute anymore." I told her I liked my sunspots
and kept walking. As I passed her cart, she said something like, "It's
a shame, you could be so pretty!"

There are right ways and wrong ways to connect your story with your customer's story. Starting with a fake compliment (or a straight-up insult) is not a great way to greet a prospect. And yet, it happens all the time. Countless unsolicited emails show up in my inbox every week offering to fix some random "problem." The thesis is always similar: "Hello! I've done research on you and think you're wonderful! However, I found out that your XYZ is broken/bad/etc. But don't fear because that's exactly what we do! We can help you fix your XYZ and everything about your life will be better in an instant!" Then, the generic, scripted funnel sequence continues for a few days.

No one wants to be approached out of the blue and told by a stranger to fix a perceived problem, whether it's in an inbox, over the phone, or in a Las Vegas shopping mall. Don't be that person. Be SUPER instead.

Bright Future in Sales

A huge percentage of us are in sales, even if our LinkedIn profiles say otherwise. I've never had a traditional "sales" job—and I've never been paid on commission—yet selling has been an instrumental part of my success at every point in my career.

When I ran the retail marketing department for a record company, the branded marketing campaigns I created resulted in millions of dollars per year in incremental revenue.

When I was an account supervisor at an advertising agency, I closed seven-figure expansion campaigns simply by taking the time to really understand my clients (and *their* customers) and suggesting creative ideas aligned with their needs.

When I launched my entertainment agency, I passed the million-dollar revenue mark in less than a year and generated millions of dollars of new business annually for almost a decade (and tens of millions in retail sales).

Finally, I went from speaking for free to getting $20,000 per keynote engagement in less than five years, all by using SUPER tactics.

Regardless of your role, you're either influencing whether the first sale will happen or whether the *next* sale will happen. Let's look at how SUPER customer experience can amplify every part of your sales process.

S | Start with your story

The more commoditized your category, the more you must focus on being the person someone wants to deal with. Lots of people can cut hair. People want the *right* hairstylist who's going to listen to their concerns and make them feel like a million bucks.

What makes *you* the absolute best person to help your prospects and customers? What makes your product or service the right solution to their problem? And, most importantly, what are you doing to ensure the entire experience, from pre-purchase to re-purchase, is one that's worth raving about?

U | Understand your customer's story

One of the most important parts of understanding your customer's story is not making *assumptions* about your customer's story.

On my most recent trip to the Apple Store, a salesperson approached and asked if he could help. I said, "I'm going to buy one of the new iPhones. I just want to hold them both to see which size I like best."

I made my selection, and the gentleman made small talk as he punched my information into his device. He told me he'd just celebrated his sixtieth birthday. Then he said, "Let me show you something. If you go to Apple.com from your mobile browser, you'll

DON'T JUST CLOSE A SALE

★ ★ CREATE ★ ★

A

SUPERFAN

find some tutorials. It's great so older folks like us don't have to ask teenagers how to use our phones."

I fought back the urge to shout, "I'm in my thirties! I know how to work an iPhone. And the spots on my face are *freckles!*"

I'm quite sure he was trying to be helpful, but his offhanded comment inadvertently sullied the entire experience. When I got home, what do you think was the first thing my husband heard about when he asked how the iPhone purchase had gone? It certainly wasn't about whatever incremental camera updates existed on the latest model.

Now, perhaps you work for a brand as big as Apple where there's enough customer loyalty to overcome the occasional thoughtless comment from a salesperson. But for most organizations, that's not the case.

P | Personalize

Never make assumptions about how any prospect or customer feels. Just like the freckles-shamer, the Apple salesperson tried to create camaraderie based on an assumed identifier.

A better way to use a potential identifier is to ask them a question. Years ago, when I was at the Capitol Records Building in Los Angeles to interview the Beach Boys for a fiftieth anniversary collaboration, I told Mike Love what an honor it was to be working with them.

Guessing by my age that I had been a kid in the '80s, he asked, "Did you watch us on *Full House* by any chance?" I said yes, and added that my dad had several Beach Boys albums in his collection and had led me down the path of full-blown fandom even before the band's sitcom cameo. Mike told me that after the band appeared on the show, the crowds at their concerts immediately became multi-generational. Suddenly, longtime fans were bringing their kids and grandkids to the shows.

The Beach Boy could tell I was hanging on every word of his *Full House* story, so he serenaded me with a rendition of their late-eighties hit "Kokomo." If I was a decade older, or if my name happened to be Rhonda or Barbara or Cindy, I'm willing to wager he would've made a different choice of which story to tell and which song to sing.

Treat each customer or prospect the way they want to be treated... not how you would want to be treated in their shoes, or how you think they *should* want to be treated based on a passing glance. Make it fun, fun, fun... and then do it again.

E | Exceed expectations

Sales unfairly gets a bad rap sometimes. It's partially because it's a blanket term used to describe countless roles and responsibilities, partially because so many people enter the workforce in sales positions with inadequate training or enablement, and partially because many people have had their trust broken at some point by an unscrupulous salesperson.

All of that said, "exceeding expectations" in sales might sometimes feel like a low bar. However, don't be tempted to barely clear the bar. Remember: *everything* is experience. Your email signature. The outgoing message on your voicemail. How early (or late) you show up for a meeting. The support you provide a customer when things go sideways. Show your love for your prospects and customers and they'll respond in kind.

R | Repeat

If you're a salesperson, your CRM is your best friend and your most powerful weapon for the "repeat" pillar of the SUPER Model. Its sole purpose is to help you make more money, yet too many salespeople don't actively use the CRMs their companies have invested big money in.

A CRM will make you more successful and free up more of your time, but only if you use it diligently. Like birth control . . . it's unbelievably effective at what it was designed to do—but only if you use it the right way, every time! And also like birth control, the largest margin of error with CRMs is due to human behavior. People forget to use it, or they think, "Oh, I don't need to use my CRM this time. Not with *this* person!" Then, a month or so later . . . surprise!

Spend the time to customize your CRM not only to fit your sales stages, but also your selling style. Create fields to capture the right information about the right people at the right time and you'll be a superfan of your CRM in a heartbeat, even if you've been resisting using it for years.

One More Time

While we're on "repeat," let's address another "R": rejection. If you're in sales, you're going to hear "no" more often than a preschool teacher at naptime.

A friend of mine once told me he was considering taking a sales job and abandoning his ambitions of starring on Broadway because, as he said, "The constant rejection is just too much for me." I laughed and told him that a sales job wasn't the escape from constant auditions and rejections that he imagined it to be!

When I launched my first startup, I was told "no" by potential clients all the time. Sometimes a dozen times a day. When it started to bum me out, I decided to flip the narrative on "no."

I wrote "NO! CHART" on a dry-erase board next to my desk. Each time a prospective customer turned me down, I drew a star on the chart. Every time I collected ten stars, I celebrated. Sometimes the celebration was as simple as having ice cream at lunch. Other times I would splurge on a nice pair of shoes or a fun top.

Each star represented someone to whom I'd told my story. Someone who now knew who I was, and what I was up to, and could put me and my company into their consideration set for the future.

Those marks didn't represent lost sales—they represented the beginning of new relationships. Someone can't share your story until they know it. They can't think of you if they don't know you exist. "No" today doesn't mean no forever.

Hard as it may be, don't get discouraged. Go back to the drawing board and personalize your next attempt with as much enthusiasm as you did your last. Repetition is the name of the game. Personalize your approach to create meaningful connections with people who, even though they aren't ready to pay for your product or service today, might be perfect customers tomorrow. The more times you tell your story, the better you'll get at it—and the more superfans you'll ultimately find.

◀◀ SUPERQUICK! REWIND ◀◀

Connecting with prospects and customers is the most important skill any salesperson can have. Identify what makes you the best person to help your customers and balance empathy and authority to learn about their wants and needs. Use your CRM to help you track personal details about your customers and ensure consistency with automation and reminders.

22

I'll Be There for You

SUPER CUSTOMER SERVICE

· · · · · · · · · · · · · · · · · · ·

Sales without customer service is like
stuffing money into a pocket full of holes.
DAVID TOOMAN

WORLD-CLASS customer service isn't cookie cutter. It isn't even about doing the same few things over and over, or simply trying to increase the convenience or efficiency or price of what your customer is expecting.

My kitchen sink was leaking recently and, as I typically do when something in the house breaks, I filed a claim on the website of my home warranty company. They dispatched a man named Perry from a local company to come diagnose the issue. After he had fixed the problem and explained it to me, he pointed up at my overhead kitchen light and said, "Now tell me, what am I looking at up there?"

The answer (brace yourself . . . this is kind of gross) was dust and a few dead bugs inside the light fixture. Something I had noticed twenty times but had never cleaned. Could I have successfully disassembled, cleaned, and re-assembled my light fixture without breaking it?

263

Probably. Had I? No. When you've got two young kids, there's always something that's more urgent.

Perry said, "Give me a ladder!" I told him it was unnecessary for him to clean my fixture (something I'm obviously capable of doing), but he insisted. When I objected a second time, he told me his mother would never approve of him not leaving something better than he found it, especially for a busy mom. He proceeded to take down the fixture, scrub it with dish soap and paper towels, dry it, climb back up the ladder, and reinstall the globe on the ceiling, all while insisting it was nothing.

That is the kind of service that turns a customer into a superfan. Regardless of the industry you're in, you're in the experience business.

Takin' Care of Business

A pet peeve of mine is how often corporate decisions are made without consulting customer service associates. There's a divide between the executives at corporate and the people working at the cash registers or answering the phones in the call center. That's why the role of chief customer officer is so important—to ensure not only that the voice of customers is being considered, but also that the voice of those *helping* the customers is amplified upward.

One of the biggest mistakes a company can make is to hire the wrong people to represent the brand. Whether it's because of a desire to fill open positions quickly or just a lack of due diligence in the hiring process, too many brands take an attitude of "anyone can do this!" and hire the first person to apply.

Some people aren't wired for customer service. It might be a lack of customer centricity, a quick temper, or a predisposition to get flustered at the first hint of conflict. Every job is important. Every employee is a living representation of your brand (remember Treadmill Delivery Guy from Chapter 3?), and it's impossible to predict what interaction might be the one that gains worldwide attention.

Here's how SUPER can power team members whose jobs involve working directly with customers.

S | Start with your story

If the most common mistake is hiring people with the wrong attitude for customer service, the second most common mistake is hiring people who lack the necessary experience or knowledge. There's nothing more frustrating for a customer than feeling like the person helping them has no idea what's going on.

If you're a software company, *every* customer-facing employee should be not just proficient, but *excellent* in your product. If you're a restaurant, your servers and hosts should have more than just a passing familiarity with your menu. When a customer asks for an opinion on choosing one steak above another, hearing a waitress say, "Oh, I'm a vegetarian" isn't helpful.

When your employees have experience with your products, services, and experiences, they can share their personal stories in ways that help connect that much more deeply with the customers. When they don't have experience, your brand *and* your team lose credibility, and customers begin wondering what shade of green the grass might be over in your competitor's backyard.

U | Understand your customer's story

Customer service employees are oftentimes the first line of defense for angry customers. When a person is annoyed or angry at the onset of an interaction, it's that much more challenging to connect with them.

Being able to read context clues—especially when you're dealing with someone on the phone or via a chat platform—can make the difference between an easy experience and an unpleasant one.

P | Personalize

Perhaps you've noticed a few of the personalizations I've pointed out in this book—hotel workers with name tags that display their hometowns, servers at a sports bar wearing the jerseys of their favorite teams, or even flight attendants whose uniforms display their years of service. Or maybe you've seen a quote or proverb in an employee's email signature, or been on the receiving end of a phone call where the help agent started by telling you their name and location. Each of these methods is designed to help share more information about the *person* behind the position, and to subtly connect their story to yours.

Of course, that's not even scratching the surface of the personalization customer-facing employees can provide. Whether it's a local barista who knows your order by heart or a gas station clerk who can read your mind when it's time to buy scratch-off lottery tickets, personal gestures of kindness go a long way. Training your team members to treat every customer as an individual will earn your brand a reputation for caring about your customers' unique needs.

E | Exceed expectations

Is seven minutes a long time to wait on hold for a customer representative? Obviously, it depends on the context. If it's an emergency call to 911, it's an eternity. If it's a Christmas Day call to an airline during a record-breaking blizzard, you'd chalk seven minutes up as a holiday miracle.

We've all been on hold and heard an automated voice say, "Your estimated wait time is nine minutes," and then still been waiting

REGARDLESS

OF THE

INDUSTRY

YOU'RE IN, YOU'RE IN

THE

EXPERIENCE

★ BUSINESS ★

fifteen minutes later. Would we have been happier to have been told fifteen minutes from the onset? For most customers, the answer is "yes."

I don't agree with the adage "under promise and over deliver." It's far better to promise what you're 99 percent certain you can deliver and then work hard to clear that bar.

R | Repeat

Repetition makes reputation, and reputation makes customers. Every interaction with every customer matters . . . even those interactions with difficult customers.

◀◀ SUPERQUICK! REWIND ◀◀

Since the customer service team is the front line of CX for many businesses, it's critically important to hire the right people and incorporate their feedback into your overall customer experience strategy. Make sure your agents are equipped with the necessary knowledge to assist customers and empower them to personalize their interactions and exceed expectations for resolution.

23

All Together Now

SUPER GLUE

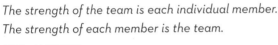

. . . .

The strength of the team is each individual member.
The strength of each member is the team.
PHIL JACKSON

W HAT IS SUPER Glue? The best adhesive ever—duh!

Just kidding. For our purposes, SUPER Glue is the collection of all departments not yet specifically addressed. The ones that, even if they have less direct interaction with customers, are helping hold the rest of the operation together.

The accounts payable team working to ensure that everyone gets paid correctly and on time. The facilities manager who makes sure the HVAC doesn't go on the fritz right before the busiest time of the year. The ops people who jump through logistical hoops all day, every day in the name of helping things run more smoothly. The legal team who helps keep everything moving in the right direction (even if they occasionally ask you to choose between "product" and "service" on a trademark application). And the countless others whose work has a direct correlation to everyone else on the team's ability to perform at the highest level possible.

Stuck Like Glue

In small or growing companies—and in a lot of family-owned businesses—many of your "glue" roles may be outside the company, with trusted vendors, contractors, or partners. Or, you may wear several sticky glue hats in addition to other roles. But just like every other aspect of the company, these departments should strive to be SUPER, too. After all, who wouldn't want to be able to brag about knowing a SUPER Model?

S | Start with your story

The more specialized your position, the less likely those outside your department are to understand it. Don't be afraid to do a little personal branding to help teach your colleagues how what you do impacts their ability to better serve customers. Things like "lunch and learn" presentations and "about me" exercises can provide additional context about your role to those around you.

U | Understand your customer's story

Which part of a customer's STORY are you most directly impacting? If you're in research and development, you may be focused on their *struggles*. If you're in the legal department, you're likely well versed on the various *reservations* a customer might have, and how to help your team overcome them. Perhaps you're an executive assistant who works tirelessly to help *transformations* come to life. Maybe you're part of the finance team, and you've got a better understanding than anyone about the *options* your customers might be considering, and how to showcase that *you* are the best in class. Everyone plays an important role in helping understand your customers.

P | Personalize

You have a uniqueness that makes you unlike anyone else. How do you bring that to the table in your position? How can that power you to improve the lives of those around you?

E | Exceed expectations

Every interaction is an opportunity to make a meaningful, memorable impression on a customer, vendor, colleague, prospect, or partner. Find ways to create as many net positive experiences as possible: Can you pay an invoice early? Deliver something sooner than promised? Provide real-time updates before you're even asked? Say "thank you" with a handwritten note? Acknowledge someone's contribution in front of a group? Set the bar high, and then systematically raise it with your actions.

R | Repeat

What are the systems and processes needed to help things run smoothly? What are the metrics that should be reviewed, and how often? Do training and enablement documents exist to help teach standard operating procedures to new team members? Don't leave the opportunity to "wow" a customer to chance; figure out how to make "wow" the standard, and then make it as easy as possible to replicate and iterate.

◄◄ SUPERQUICK! REWIND ◄◄

Even if you're not working directly with customers every day, your actions impact them and their satisfaction with your company. The "glue" roles that hold together the rest of the departments play an important role in CX because they're the foundation upon which customer promises are built.

24

Never Really Over

SUPER FUTURE

. . . .

*There is no real ending. It's just
the place where you stop the story.*

FRANK HERBERT

WERE YOU the kid who always asked your teacher for homework on the last day of school so you'd have something to do over the summer? No? Just me?

If you haven't already done so, go to BrittanyHodak.com/SUPER to download your free copy of the Creating Superfans Playbook. Thousands of people have credited it with amplifying their businesses in a *huge* way, and I want that for you, too.

Think of it like the encore at the end of the concert. The show isn't complete without it . . . and it might just be your favorite part. (Cue "Gimme More" singalong!)

I can't tell you the number of times I've read a book and felt inspired, only to have that excitement and momentum die down in a couple of days. Or, to have it be replaced by a new fire when I started a different book.

273

Don't let this be the end. Make it the beginning.

Adopt the SUPER Model as your new mantra. Shout it from the rooftops the same way you sang some of the songs whose titles I snuck in here. (That's right, I heard you!) Rally everyone in your orbit around turning your customers into superfans.

I've curated numerous resources to support you on your journey. If you're looking for more personalized support, you'll find information at BrittanyHodak.com about my speaking, consulting, and video course offerings. Each is designed to make amazing customer experience your company's biggest competitive advantage.

Want to empower everyone in your team or organization with the secrets of creating superfans? Say no more! Volume discounts are available for bulk purchases. Please email Books@BrittanyHodak.com for more information.

This book wasn't created to be a one-way conversation. If you have thoughts, requests, questions, or anything else to share, say hi at Hello@BrittanyHodak.com, or tag your social messages with #superfans. No mean tweets, please—save those for Jimmy Kimmel!

If you're feeling generous, please take sixty seconds to review this book on your favorite website or tell a friend or librarian about it. It would mean a lot to me, and it will help more super-fantastic people like you discover it.

I know there are countless other things you could've done with the time you spent reading this book, and I'm grateful you chose to spend it with me. Thank you.

As my favorite after-school superhero Captain Planet would say, "The power is yours!" I can't wait to see what SUPER things you do with it.

Exitlude

ONE DAY, a few weeks before my oldest son turned three, he ran into my office while I was writing. I gently reminded him that I was working on this book and asked him to go back downstairs to play with Daddy.

With a look of genuine interest he asked, "What's your book about, Mommy?"

I paused for a second, then tried to explain the concept of *Creating Superfans* in a way a preschooler would understand. When I noticed his attention trailing I asked, "What do you think?"

I expected him to suggest I write about something more fun, like dinosaurs or construction vehicles. Instead, he was silent for a second, as if gathering his thoughts. He looked me right in the eyes and said, "I think you should tell all the people to be nice and listen."

Mic drop.

After he shared his preschool wisdom, he danced out of the room like it was nothing.

"Be nice and listen."

It's solid advice. Although I guess I shouldn't be surprised that a kid whose full name is a palindrome has a gift for words.

Be nice and listen. Be SUPER. Put your customers first and I guarantee those customers will last.

"**BE NICE**

★★★ **AND** ★★★

LISTEN"

— **KADOH HODAK** —

Thank Yous

Thank You for Being a Friend

In case I never win a Grammy (although you'd better believe I'm submitting the audiobook version of this book for the Recording Academy's consideration), I want to thank a few of the wonderful people who've immeasurably improved my life and this project.

Thank you to my husband, Jeff, the best friend and partner anyone could ask for. Thanks to our terrific boys, Kadoh and Jones, for making me laugh and for giving me (semi-)quiet time to write this book. You're my three favorite people in the world!

Thanks to my dad, Jody, for teaching me that there's nothing more important than the way you treat people and for inspiring my obsession with customer experience. Thanks to my mom, Kenda, for inspiring my love of writing and reading, and for driving me to the library and back hundreds of times.

Thanks to my brother, Brandon, for setting annoyingly high standards to chase at school and at home, and for bringing Hailey and Dawn into our family.

Thanks to my grandparents, Marilyn, Bud, Gina, and Harry; my mother-in-law, Maria; my father-in-law, Ron; my amazing cousins

(Justin, Tiffany, Jennifer, Zachary, Rachel, Jessica, Dustin, Emily, Chelsea, and Luke), aunts (Vicki, Gwen, Rhonda, and Lindy), uncles (Ken and Terry), and extended family members on the Jones and Hodak sides for a lifetime of love and support.

Thank you to Shep Hyken for blazing a path for CX enthusiasts like me, for sharing the kind words in this book's foreword, and for teaching me so much, onstage and off. I was your superfan long before you had any idea I existed. I'm lucky to have you as my adopted uncle!

Thank you to the two MVPs on my team for your help every day: Alix Steinberg and Grace Fershee.

Thank you to the incomparable team at Page Two, including Trena White, Jesse Finkelstein, Rony Ganon, Emily Schultz, Melissa Edwards, Alison Strobel, Peter Cocking, Fiona Lee, Chris Brandt, Madelaine Manson, and Lorraine Toor for helping bring this book—and my lifelong dream of being an author—to life. You've been amazing at every (page) turn.

Thank you to the most inspiring friends imaginable for making life more fun, including Pamela Roberts, Rose Gulferi Dunn, John Hall, Joey Coleman, Travis and Jaden Sutliff, Rory and AJ Vaden, Bridget Hilton, Annie Reuter, Rachel Sheerin, Rachel DeAlto, and Emily Yahr.

I'm so grateful for all the clients, coaches, colleagues, and champions who've become dear friends and advisors over the years. I owe a huge debt of gratitude to so many, including Sam and Beth Alex, Elyse Archer, Jane Atkinson, Ethan Beute, Karen Blakeslee, Susie Bonner, Jacquie Brink, Margaret Brittingham, Katherine Caraway, Matt Clarke, Clayton Collins, Cassie Croft, Faithe Dillman, Grace and Brian Dolan, James Duncan, Jason Frazell, Gino Fronti, Jeff Glover, Don Goettling, Fawn Goodman, Scott Harris, Cheryl Hayes, Angela Higgins, Jon Hill, Traci Huntemann-Piatt, Lloyd Hummel, Norman Hurd, Kelly Kastel, Kelly Rich Kautz, Cecil Kemp, Taylor Kerrigan, Greg Lambert,

Michael Lawson, Eric Levin, Tamika Ligon, Gene Lugat, Matt Lyles, Andrea Malis, Mira Mambetalieva, Rebecca Martin, Michael Maturo, Kristin Messerli, Kelsey Meyer, Suzy Mills, Arel Moodie, Sue Nester, Zack O'Malley Greenburg, Cece and Taylorr Payne, Cassie Petrey, Josh Pitts, John Rampton, Laurie Rauen, Jenni Readio, Macy Robison, John Ruhlin, Traci Saliterman, Dave Savage, Eric Skates, Chris Sorensen, Justin Stutz, Phil Treadwell, Justin Tucker, Chris West, Sarah Wheeler, Sue Woodward, Frank Woodworth, Melissa Wright, and Jim Zumwalt.

Thank you to the recording artists, record executives, and brand clients who believed in me and helped me build my businesses over the past two decades. It's been thrilling and humbling to work alongside all of you.

Thank you to all of the authors, speakers, comedians, and creators whose work has inspired me over the years, either from up close or afar.

Thank you to everyone who so graciously allowed me to share your stories in this book, and to the companies whose unwavering commitment to customer centricity helped shape it.

Thank you to everyone who was kind enough to offer a review for this book ahead of its release ... and to everyone who takes the time to review it, share it, or talk about it now that it's out in the world.

Most of all, thank YOU for reading this. I've loved books since before I was old enough to read the words in them and I have dreamed about writing my own for as long as I can remember. I hope this one has earned a spot among your favorites and sparked a passion for turning customers into superfans.

Credits

6: My List

p. 77 *80 percent of customers said the experience a company provides matters as much*... Salesforce Research, "State of the Connected Customer, Second Edition," 2018, salesforce.com/content/dam/web/en_us/www/documents/e-books/state-of-the-connected-customer-report-second-edition2018.pdf.

p. 88 *Jon proposes this simple framework for overcoming negative thoughts*... Jon Acuff, *Soundtracks: The Surprising Solution to Overthinking* (Baker Books, 2021).

7: The STORY of Us

p. 96 *I've talked to nearly 30,000 people on this show*... Oprah Winfrey, "The Oprah Winfrey Show Finale," *The Oprah Winfrey Show*, season 25, episode 131, aired on May 25, 2011.

9: I Want You to Want Me

p. 125 *71 percent of consumers expect companies to deliver personalized interactions*... McKinsey & Company, "The Value of Getting Personalization Right—or Wrong—Is Multiplying," *Next in Personalization 2021 Report*, November 12, 2021, mckinsey.com/business-functions/growth-marketing-and-sales/our-insights/the-value-of-getting-personalization-right-or-wrong-is-multiplying.

p. 128 *Alessandra's Platinum Rule takes the Golden Rule a step further*... Tony Alessandra and Michael O'Connor, *The Platinum Rule: Discover the Four Basic Business Personalities—and How They Can Lead You to Success* (Grand Central Publishing, 1998).

11: All the Small Things

p. 153 *New York–based author and artist Craig Damrauer summed up modern art*... Craig Damrauer, *New Math*, assortedbitsofwisdom.com/New-Math-1.

13: Back 2 Good

p. 181 *The term "service recovery paradox" was first used in 1992*... Michael McCollough and Sundar Bharadwaj, "The Recovery Paradox: An Examination of Customer Satisfaction in Relation to Disconfirmation, Service Quality, and Attribution Based Theories," in *Marketing Theory and Applications*, edited by Chris T. Allen (American Marketing Association, 1992).

14: Here I Go Again

p. 197   *Rory Vaden suggests asking yourself these questions about every task on your to-do list* . . . Rory Vaden, "How to Multiply Your Time," TEDxDouglasville, June 1, 2015, roryvaden.com/blog-posts/rory-vaden-ted-talk.

16: Pet Sounds

p. 219   *In its first year, Chewy did about $26 million in sales* . . . Emily Canal, "Meet the Young Founders of Chewy.com, Which PetSmart Just Bought for $3.35 Billion," *Inc.*, April 19, 2017, inc.com/emily-canal/petsmart-acquires-chewy.html.

p. 221   *Now, here's some language in the company's own words* . . . Chewy, "Corporate Overview," investor.chewy.com/overview.

17: Come as You Are

p. 226   *This is directly from the Finnleys website* . . . Finnleys, finnleysonline.com.

18: Ain't No Stoppin' Us Now

p. 233   *Shonda Rhimes was producing nearly seventy hours of content for ABC* . . . Lacey Rose, "Shonda Rhimes Is Ready to 'Own Her S***': The Game-Changing Showrunner on Leaving ABC, 'Culture Shock' at Netflix and Overcoming Her Fears," *Hollywood Reporter*, October 21, 2020, hollywoodreporter.com/movies/movie-features/shonda-rhimes-is-ready-to-own-her-s-the-game-changing-showrunner-on-leaving-abc-culture-shock-at-netflix-and-overcoming-her-fears-4079375.

p. 236   *He explained that the chain hires nice people and treats them well* . . . Tara Miller and Matt Sloan, hosts, "Why Is Everyone So Nice?" *Inside Trader Joe's* podcast, Episode 14, May 20, 2019, traderjoes.com/content/dam/trjo/pdfs/transcript-pdfs/InsideTJs-Episode14-Transcript.pdf.

20: Show Me What You Got

p. 252   *According to* Adweek, *Allstate's "You're in good hands" slogan was born in 1950* . . . Mae Anderson, "53 Years Later, Still in Good Hands," *Adweek*, February 3, 2003, adweek.com/brand-marketing/53-years-later-still-good-hands-61449.

Bonus Tracks

Ch-Check It Out

Sometimes when an artist records an album, a few of their favorite tracks get left on the cutting room floor. It isn't (always) because they aren't great, but sometimes a song just doesn't fit anywhere on the album.

Writing a book is the same way. There were hundreds of stories, studies, examples, and statistics I wanted to include but couldn't. I invite you to check out BrittanyHodak.com/BonusTracks, where you'll find several future fan favorites, including:

- An always-up-to-date list of my favorite books and podcasts so you can enjoy them, too.

- Video resources to help amplify the SUPER Model at every level of your organization.

- Surprises so good I'm not going to tell you here! Go check 'em out— you'll be glad you did.

BrittanyHodak.com/BonusTracks

Tour Dates

On the Road Again

Want to hang out in real life? Me too! I'm always on tour, giving entertaining, high-energy keynotes packed with actionable takeaways to help organizations big and small create superfans.

I accept about forty in-person speaking invitations per year, plus virtual events and a limited number of consulting engagements, from some of the greatest brands in the world.

Find out why amazing companies like American Express, *Forbes*, HousingWire, Total Expert, and PrimeLending have invited me back again and again at **BrittanyHodak.com/Speaking.**

About the Author

Hello, It's Me

BRITTANY HODAK is an award-winning entrepreneur, speaker, and author who has delivered keynotes across the globe to organizations including American Express and the United Nations. She has written hundreds of articles for *Forbes*, *Adweek*, *Success*, and other top publications; she has appeared on programs on NBC, CBS, ABC, and FOX; and she has worked with some of the world's biggest brands and entertainers, including Walmart, Disney, Katy Perry, and Dolly Parton. *Entrepreneur* calls her "the expert at creating loyal fans for your brand." Brittany is unapologetically obsessed with customer experience and, more than anything, she hopes *you* are a superfan of this book.

We Should Be Friends

@BrittanyHodak | Hello@BrittanyHodak.com | BrittanyHodak.com